W9-AUD-773

Also by Alan C. Greenberg

MEMOS FROM THE CHAIRMAN

THE
RISE
AND
FALL
OF
BEAR STEARNS

ALAN C. GREENBERG
WITH MARK SINGER

SIMON & SCHUSTER
NEW YORK LONDON TORONTO SYDNEY

Simon & Schuster
1230 Avenue of the Americas
New York, NY 10020

First Simon & Schuster hardcover edition June 2010

SIMON & SCHUSTER and colophon are registered
trademarks of Simon & Schuster, Inc.

For information about special discounts for bulk purchases,
please contact Simon & Schuster Special Sales at
1-800-456-6798 or business@simonandschuster.com.

Designed by C. Linda Dingler

Manufactured in the United States of America

10 9 8 7 6 5 4 3 2 1

Library of Congress Cataloging-in-Publication Data

Greenberg, Alan C.
  The rise and fall of Bear Stearns / Alan C. Greenberg
with Mark Singer.
    p. cm.
    Includes index.
    1. Bear, Stearns & Co.—History—21st century.   2. Investment
banking—United States—21st century.   3. Subprime mortgage
loans—United States—21st century.   4. Financial crises—United
States—21st century.   I. Singer, Mark.   II. Title.
HG4930.5.G74 2010
332.660973—dc22   2010005141

ISBN 978-1-4165-6288-7
ISBN 978-1-4391-0973-1 (ebook)

To Kathy, Lynne, and Teddy

THE
RISE
AND
FALL
OF
BEAR STEARNS

CHAPTER

1

ON MARCH 16, 2008, I WAS AT WORK AT Bear Stearns, but in a distinct departure from my usual routine. For one thing, it was a Sunday, and the last time I had worked weekends was during the 1950s, when the stock market had Saturday trading hours. This particular Sunday was drizzly and gray—fitting weather (actually, a squall with golf-ball-size hail plus an earthquake would have been more like it) for confronting a calamity that even in my gloomiest risk calculations I hadn't seen coming. Shortly before noon, I went to our headquarters at 383 Madison Avenue for an emergency meeting of the corporate board of directors. The week just ended had been the most maddening, bizarre, and bewildering in our eighty-five-year history.

Occasional bad news is inevitable, but I've tried to order my life to avoid getting blindsided. Sixty-one years ago I moved to New York and found work as a clerk at Bear Stearns, an investment firm that had 125 employees. Before I turned forty, I was running the place. At its peak, Bear Stearns employed almost 15,000 people. Along the way, my formal titles included chief executive officer, chairman, and chairman of the executive committee; my principal occupation was and continues to be calculating and managing risks.

My workday typically started off like this: out the door by

8:00 a.m. and at my desk by 8:15, where my morning reading consisted of the *Wall Street Journal*—at home I'd already digested the *New York Times* and the New York *Post*—and printed reports that specified how various departments that handled the firm's capital had performed the previous day. If a trader had an especially good day, I'd probably call to congratulate him. If the opposite occurred, I'd want to find out what happened. Before the markets opened at 9:30, I'd usually handled more than a dozen phone calls. As the day progressed, I'd be easy to get hold of but hard to keep on the line. Most phone conversations that last longer than thirty seconds, I find, have reached a point of diminishing returns. I have many interests and hobbies, but making small talk isn't one of them.

Anyone who invests money and neglects to calculate the risks at hand with a cold eye has no business being in our business. Contrary to common belief, securities markets are not casinos, and the last thing I ever want to depend upon is getting lucky. The best risk managers instinctively anticipate the fullest range of plausible outcomes. Maintaining that discipline, I understood early on, was indispensable to long-term success.

It would be disingenuous to suggest that making money is not a reasonable way of keeping score. For any financial institution, it's obviously the essential priority. But I never regarded making money, either when Bear Stearns was a private partnership or after it became a public company, as an end in itself. The more Bear Stearns flourished, the greater the variety of products and services we offered our clients, the more our capital grew, the more people we employed, and thus the more families that depended upon the well-being of the enterprise, the deeper was my conviction that we existed, above all, for the purpose of existing. On any given day, my *ultimate* priority was that we conduct ourselves so that Bear Stearns would still be in business tomorrow.

THE PREVIOUS Monday morning our stock price had begun dropping, and by noon it was off 10 percent, from $70 to $63 a share. Part of this decline was attributable to Moody's, the bond-rating agency, having just downgraded some of our corporate debt. But most of the damage was being inflicted by a much more insidious factor, a groundless rumor. (Do rumors come from the same neighborhood where the notorious *they* hold their conspiratorial get-togethers?) This one surfaced first in feedback picked up by some of our traders: Bear Stearns, so it was being said on the Street, had liquidity problems. In other words, we might not have enough capital or credit to fund our daily operations—the billions of dollars of trades that we processed and settled for our biggest clients, including banks, mutual funds, hedge funds, pension funds, and insurance companies.

The interdependent relationships between banks and brokerages and institutional investors strike most laymen as impenetrably complex, but a simple ingredient lubricates the engine: trust. Without reciprocal trust between the parties to any securities transaction, the money stops. Doubt fills the vacuum, and credit and liquidity are the chief casualties. Bad news, whether it derives from false rumor or verifiable fact, then has an alarming capacity to become contagious and self-perpetuating. No problem is an isolated problem.

The sharp decline in our stock price was plenty disturbing— a billion dollars of market capitalization had evaporated, like that. But no one that I was aware of at Bear Stearns had begun to panic, largely because for several months disappointment had been a staple of our diet. In the summer of 2007, two of our real estate hedge funds failed, a fiasco that cost us $1 billion and did not exactly enhance the firm's reputation. This part of our business in recent years had accounted for a large percentage of our trading volume and an equally large percentage of profits, but as the real estate bubble deflated our inventory of distressed assets inflated—a highly leveraged portfolio of mortgage-backed securities that was a drag on our balance sheet and our morale. In the fourth quarter, we recorded our first loss since becoming a publicly owned company in 1985. Still, in the quarter just ended, though the results hadn't yet been officially announced, we had turned a small profit—not great, but better than a minus sign. And as far as liquidity was concerned, we had a cash reserve of $18 billion.

What we didn't have was any ability to stifle the rumors, which were no longer being whispered but broadcast on the financial-news cable channels. When a reporter from CNBC called to ask about alleged liquidity problems, I told her that the notion was "totally ridiculous." That comment got broadcast, too, but evidently didn't do much good. The next day a number of hedge funds closed their accounts and by the following afternoon our cash reserve was more than $3 billion lighter. By Thursday enough lenders had cut off our access to overnight credit that we confronted an excruciating choice—either a shotgun marriage with another firm that would assume our liabilities while swallowing what remained of Bear Stearns's equity, or a bankruptcy filing. When the market closed for the weekend, our stock was trading in the low thirties—fourteen months earlier, it had peaked at $172.69—and we knew that come Monday we would have been bought or we would be no more. Without a doubt, we would never again control our own destiny.

Throughout the weekend swarms of bankers and investment bankers and mergers-and-acquisition lawyers and bankruptcy lawyers and tax and securities specialists, as well as officials from the Federal Reserve Bank and the Department of the Treasury, worked round the clock. Two potential buyers scrutinized our books and both were handicapped by an inability to judge the magnitude of risk. For starters, which of our assets were genuine assets? How do you ascribe values to unmarketable securities? By Sunday morning only JPMorgan Chase remained. When I left home for the directors' meeting, I anticipated that I was on my way to contemplate whatever offer Morgan had placed on the table. By the time I arrived, the offer had been withdrawn, and I was advised that I might as well go home. Which is where I was a half-hour later when I got another call, urging me to come back.

Our board of directors convened at 1:00 p.m., six hours before the Monday morning opening of the markets in Australia—the absolute deadline for making a deal. If Bear Stearns went under, the Fed and Treasury had insisted, the falling dominoes could lead to global economic chaos. Only after the Treasury had agreed to lend $30 billion, using as collateral the highest-quality mortgage-backed securities in Bear Stearns's portfolio, did Morgan's leadership find that line of argument persuasive. (Quid pro quo, the Fed—that is, American taxpayers—stood to make a profit if those securities could later be sold at a premium, and Morgan agreed to absorb the first billion dollars of potential losses.) The biggest losers, obviously, would be Bear Stearns's stockholders. The previous day, we'd been led to expect that Morgan would bid in the range of $8 to $12 a share, but that was yesterday. Now Alan Schwartz, our chief executive officer, told us to brace ourselves for a price closer to $4.

His predecessor, James E. (Jimmy) Cayne, who was still the chairman of the board—but who would have been in Detroit playing in a bridge tournament if Alan hadn't convinced him to return to New York—was furious. At $4 a share, he argued, why not just file for bankruptcy? A few other people in the room shared Jimmy's sense of frustration, but he was by far the most vehement. On the face of it, his reaction was understandable: he owned 5.66 million shares, a stake that had once been worth more than a billion dollars. But did his outrage reflect primarily a concern for his own well-being—I felt confident that Jimmy himself would still be able to pay the grocery and electric and rent bills—or that of our employees?

What I knew for certain was that bankruptcy would mean liquidation, an outcome to be avoided at virtually any cost. A very high proportion of Bear Stearns's personnel had invested the bulk of their life savings in Bear Stearns stock. Liquidation would render the stock worthless and put more than 14,000 people on the street.

The mood in the boardroom didn't improve when the formal, final bid from Morgan materialized. They were offering *two* dollars, not four. That offer put the total value of the company, with enormous contingent liabilities built into the price, at $263 million, or roughly one-quarter of the market value of our most valuable illiquid asset, our forty-two-story corporate headquarters.

"I am *not* taking $2," Jimmy said.

"Jimmy, if we don't take $2 we'll get zero," I told him. "If they're only offering fifty cents we should take it because it means we're still alive. When you're dead nothing can happen to you except you'll go to heaven or hell, maybe. You want us to declare bankruptcy this evening?"

He didn't say anything else that I recall; not that there was much else to be said at that moment. Though we barely beat the 7:00 deadline, we did, in fact, make a deal. You could argue that we'd undergone a multiple organ transplant and were on life support. Or that, one-upping Dr. Frankenstein, several of our healthy organs had been grafted to another body. Either way, parts of us were still alive. A half hour after the vote, I got into a taxi and went home, feeling both heartsick and relieved. In the morning, I'd be back at my desk.

Nothing that had occurred that day or that week undermined my belief in the management principles and investing discipline I'd lived by throughout my career. But there was no escaping that what qualified in my world as a cataclysmic event had taken place, and none of us could confidently predict the particulars of what would come next. Our most unassailable assumption—that Bear Stearns, an independent investment firm with a proud eighty-five-year history, would be in business tomorrow—had been extinguished. How were we to envision the future? What *was* it, exactly, that had happened, and how, and why?

CHAPTER

2

GREENBERG'S THEORY OF RELATIVITY: There's timing, and then there's timing.

Corollary: You're never as smart as you might think you are on a good day. On a very bad one, you're probably not as dumb as you fear you are.

When I was twenty-one years old, in 1948, I had a notion that seemed reasonable: leave home, get a job on Wall Street, make a bunch of money. After a year at the Unviversity of Oklahoma, I'd transferred to the University of Missouri, where I was about to complete a degree in business and management. An important influence at that point was my extracurricular reading about the Gilded Age and its legacy. I'd become fascinated with the leading protagonists, figures like Jay Gould, J. P. Morgan, Jim Fisk, and Jacob Schiff—for their work ethics, talents for recognizing opportunities, steady wisdom in the face of uncertainty, and clarity when confronting a Big Picture. For similar reasons, I was also in awe of Bernard Baruch. (I confess that my admiration for Baruch dimmed many years later, when my friend Kitty Carlisle Hart told me how he'd once invited her to his plantation in South Carolina for a hunting trip. Baruch's idea of hunting, she found out, bore no resemblance to hers.) It was these men's roles as public citizens, and especially in the case of Schiff, his philanthropy, that impressed me most. I was amazed that Schiff, a German-Jewish immigrant who never lost his heavy accent, had been able to compete with the likes of J. P. Morgan.

As for timing, mine could have been better. Through a friend of my father's, in the fall of 1948 I'd been offered a job at P. F. Fox, a small brokerage firm that specialized in over-the-counter oil-and-gas stocks. But the market had been in a rut for months, and before Christmas I was told sorry, no job. Still, I intended to go to New York, and in February 1949, right after I graduated from Missouri a semester early, my parents and my younger brother and sister, Maynard and DiAnne, saw me off at the train station in Oklahoma City. As my father told me good-bye, he handed me a check for $3,000 and said, "This is it." When the train pulled away my mother cried and said, "We'll never see Alan in Oklahoma again." This was overly dramatic but not necessarily pessimistic. She might not have known, but I did, that I could wind up back on that train platform in time to see the redbuds blossom.

That passenger on the Santa Fe Railroad—who *was* he? Forgive me for omitting heartrending details of my childhood traumas, but I can't think of any. I had a remarkably pleasant upbringing. Someone once asked my mother whether I'd been an easy or difficult child to raise and she said, "Very difficult. You think it's easy to deal with a four-year-old who's smarter than you?" Much as I'm reluctant to impugn her credibility, my recollection is that we got along swell.

My parents, Ted Greenberg and Esther Zeligson, were first-generation American-born Jews of the Midwestern diaspora, children of Russian and Polish immigrants. He came from Kansas City by way of Evansville, Indiana; she was born in Sioux City, Iowa, and grew up in Nebraska and Oklahoma. They met in Tulsa in 1924, and married a year later—he was twenty, she was eighteen. They set up housekeeping briefly in Topeka, Kansas—Dad later claimed that Topeka had no indoor plumbing—and then in Wichita. When I entered the picture, two years later, he was operating a successful ladies' ready-to-wear store. Across the border, in Oklahoma, oil discoveries had proliferated for a couple of decades. What really got his attention was the wildcat well that opened the great Oklahoma City field in 1928.

My father had more common sense than anyone I've ever met (Warren Buffett is a not-too-distant second), and he knew that his business prospects in Wichita couldn't compete with whatever an oil boomtown had to offer. The year I turned five our family moved to Oklahoma City. Eventually his business, Street's, a clothing store catering mostly to women, expanded to eleven stores. For the next sixty years it comfortably supported six families of Greenberg brothers—Ted, despite being the youngest, was boss—and many of their offspring.

My tenure there didn't last long. When I was fifteen I had a part-time job in the credit department of the flagship store downtown. Qualifying for credit back then was, let's say, significantly more demanding than it would later become. The lowest-risk variety that Street's offered was layaway buying; a customer found an item he or she wanted to buy, paid in installments, and the merchandise left the store only after it had been fully paid for. One morning a woman who had a dress on layaway came in and made a $20 payment. In the afternoon she returned to make a final payment. This seemed odd, I mentioned it to the office manager and, what do you know, she'd mistakenly been credited for a $200 payment and was trying to pull a fast one. "I'm taking the rest of the afternoon off," I told the manager. "I've done what I can for the day. Saved the store $180." That was my biggest achievement at Street's.

Among the factual errors I came across in journalistic accounts of JPMorgan's takeover of Bear Stearns, one of the most aggravating was a blind quote in *Vanity Fair* describing me on the day the rumors of a liquidity problem went public as "kind of freaking out that morning." Put it this way: the last time I freaked out was in fourth grade, 1936, when my mother made me wear knickers to school. We were part of an influx of affluent families into Crown Heights, a newly developed area of spacious and smartly landscaped brick and sandstone houses. A few years earlier this part of Oklahoma City had been a nameless rural expense populated by farm families that were barely getting by. Many of my classmates still lived on farms. Before fourth grade I'd always worn long pants. For some reason, my mother couldn't understand how knickers might be a serious social liability in a school where many of the other kids didn't have shoes.

The school was Horace Mann and its principal, Everett Marshall, was someone we all liked a lot. About twenty years ago, when he was dying, he asked his son to get in touch with my brother and tell him that our father, who died in 1980, had anonymously bought shoes for the poor kids at Horace Mann and had made Mr. Marshall promise to keep that a secret. This revelation pleased but hardly surprised us. Not all of Dad's charitable deeds were anonymous, but he and Ev Marshall shared an aversion to self-aggrandizement. At least one of Mr. Marshall's egalitarian convictions, I have to say, didn't sit well with me. Because some kids couldn't afford softball gloves, he refused to let any of us wear them—except the catcher, and Mr. Marshall paid for that one. When we played teams from other schools, they had gloves and we didn't. We usually managed to win anyway.

Before I began plotting my course as a ruthless capitalist, sports were my principal enthusiasm and football was my favorite. Occasionally I've wondered how good a player I might have become if I hadn't had to go to Hebrew school four days a week until I was thirteen. My high school, Classen, had a history teacher who was also the assistant football coach. I was number one in his class by about a mile, and he liked me. I went out for spring football practice during my sophomore year. The first day, about fifty guys had their hands in the air, hoping the coach would let them show what they could do. Because he already knew me, I got the first shot—a big break. I might have gotten noticed anyway, but that made it easier. Spring football amounted to thirty days of brutal action—we scrimmaged every day—and the coaches didn't much care if you got hurt because you had all summer to heal. I became a second-string halfback. My father came to a scrimmage and after seeing the first-stringer in action asked me, "That guy Jimmy Owens—you play the same position, right?" I said yes.

"And he's the same year as you, isn't he?"

"Yes."

"You either need to quit or change positions." Jimmy went on to become captain of the University of Oklahoma football team that went undefeated and won the Sugar Bowl in 1949. Turned out my father was right about that, too.

At the end of the spring I weighed 148 pounds, which I thought was too small, so I went on an eating binge. My mother thought it was a tribute to her cooking, but watching me eat made Dad sick. By fall I was up to 171 pounds—I'd spent the summer unloading trucks, mainly for the body-building benefits—but it didn't affect my speed.

In the spring I also ran track. If you met me today that might not be your first impression, but you could look it up. I ran a ten-seconds-flat 100-yard dash, and my junior and senior years I won the city and district championships in the 100 and the 220 and finished fourth and third, respectively, in the state championship meet. Also during my senior year, our football team won the state championship, and I had a reputation as the fastest high school running back in Oklahoma. The University of Oklahoma offered me a football scholarship, I enrolled in the fall of 1945, had a very good first game, and then seriously injured my back in our second game, against Nebraska. That ended my football career and precipitated my transfer to the University of Missouri—if I wasn't going to play football, I wanted to be further than eighteen miles from home—which in turn precipitated a slight alteration in my identity.

Boys outnumbered girls five to one at Missouri, and most of my male classmates were five years older than me because they'd served in the Second World War. One of my roommates, Jay Sarno, who went on to become one of the major casino developers in Las Vegas—he came up with the ideas for and built both Caesars Palace and Circus Circus—said to me, "Greenberg, you're not a bad-looking guy. But with a name like yours you're not going to get anywhere socially." So he decided I should call myself Ace Gainsboro. A few days later I reverted to Greenberg, but the Ace stuck. If that's somehow worked to my disadvantage over the years, I haven't noticed.

When it came to introducing myself to prospective employers, I was still Alan. I don't think that worked to my disadvantage either, though the first several firms I called on did find me resistible. A very successful oilman from Wichita named Nate Appleman, who also later moved to New York, had given me six letters of introduction that said, "I don't know Alan but I know his uncle. Anything you can do to help him would be appreciated." My father had told me to stay at a nice hotel, so I did—the Tuscany, on Thirty-eighth Street. Every weekday morning I put on a suit and tie and went to the office of P. F. Fox, on lower Broadway. Freddy Fox, the owner, felt badly about rescinding his job offer and let me use a desk and a phone while I looked for work. His secretary, Hazel, loved to hear me talk, couldn't get over my Oklahoma twang, so I provided some entertainment value.

The only person I knew in New York was a girl I'd met during summer school at the University of Wisconsin. I thought she could be my guide, but when I called the first thing she told me was, "I just got engaged." One weekend I went to the Winter Antiques Show, met a cute-looking girl, and talked her into having one date with me. Otherwise, I was quite on my own. The weather was much colder than I'd been accustomed to, and I wound up spending a lot of time at the main branch of the New York Public Library, a nice warm place with clean bathrooms and every book in the world. I went there every day and mostly read books about magic (a lifelong passion that began when I was eight years old and saw the Great Blackstone perform in Oklahoma City). In the years to come, the gifts I was able to make to the Library brought me as much pleasure as any of my philanthropic bequests.

The letters from Nate Appleman got me in the door at several Wall Street firms that, not coincidentally, were predominantly Jewish: Wertheim, Carl M. Loeb, Rhoades & Co., Sartorius, Bache, H. Hentz, and Bear Stearns. Everybody told me to go back to Oklahoma—until I visited Bear Stearns, which by chance was doing fairly well. I happened to have shown up at a time when there was an opening in the oil-

and-gas department, as an assistant to Mr. Dickson. (His first name was Leonard, but I never heard anyone call him that.) No explanation of what my duties would be, but I liked that it was a job. It paid $135 a month and I could start work the following Monday, which I proceeded to do. That day, March 8, 1949, the trading volume on the New York Stock Exchange totaled 800,000 shares. The Dow closed at 180.

3

THE BEAR STEARNS THAT I WENT TO work for was a steadily profitable, though by white-shoe standards less than prestigious, enterprise that had been around since 1923. It had an impressive-sounding address— 1 Wall Street—if you were impressed by that sort of thing, but the offices were nothing special. You stepped off the elevator on the sixteenth floor into a dark-paneled, dimly lit reception area and were greeted by an elderly man wearing a blue smock. The main trading room was about 1,000 square feet and furnished with wooden desks that looked like they belonged in an English boarding school. Each telephone had a stiff cord and a direct connection to our competitors: Goldman Sachs, Josephthal & Co., Abraham & Co., Lehman Bros., Carl M. Loeb, Rhoades & Co., and others. (Only one of which, by the way, Goldman Sachs, is still in business, and even Goldman Sachs, which is now officially chartered as a state bank, appeared to have a near-death experience in the fall of 2008.) About a dozen desks in a partitioned area of the room were occupied by retail sales representatives. The municipal bond department consisted of three traders, and there were six or eight equity and corporate bond traders. A steady flow of ticker tape inched from a terminal at one end of a side-by-side row of desks and got read by every trader along the way. A retail rep who had a client on the phone would know the last trading price of a stock or a bond but needed to be told the current bid. "What's the market?" he would shout, a question that a clerk would relay to one of our traders on the floor of the stock exchange. You've undoubtedly seen this movie before.

Frustratingly, for what seemed like a very long while none of it had much to do with me. The job I'd enlisted for in the oil-and-gas department, which consisted entirely of Mr. Dickson and me, was laughably tedious. If only I'd found it funny. On one wall Mr. Dickson had mounted a very large map of the United States and my primary responsibility was to decorate it with straight pins. First, I'd consult the most recent issue of the *Oil & Gas Journal*, gleaning progress reports of exploration activity wherever it existed, and then I'd stick a color-coded pin in the corresponding spot on the map. I had been at this about eleven minutes on Day One when it occurred to me that my abilities weren't being fully tested.

I enjoyed a brief respite in the form of a two-week training period, a rotation through various departments. One morning while I was assigned to purchase-and-sales, I saw a huddle of back-office people discussing a huge trade that had just gone through, a million shares of Investor Diversified Services, of Minneapolis. The previous day, Cy Lewis, the head of the firm, had bought it for our account and promptly granted an option to buy it for a half point above our cost to Robert Young, a railroad tycoon who owned a controlling interest in the Allegheny Corporation. So now Young had exercised the option and Bear Stearns had turned a $500,000 overnight profit. This little eye-opener certainly captured my attention and imagination (never mind that, long-term, Young probably wound up with a $50 million profit). Anyway, the next thing I knew I was back jabbing colored pins into a map.

At lunchtime every day I would eat quickly and run into the trading room and station myself as inconspicuously as possible while I watched and listened. For any Wall Street firm to be very busy in those days was unusual. That Bear Stearns happened to be was due in large part to its sophistication at risk arbitrage—buying or short-selling positions in companies that were parties to proposed mergers.

The partner who ran the department was John Slade, then in the prime of a Bear Stearns career that spanned sixty-five years. The day that he finally noticed me, he asked, "Are you a client?" No, I was a clerk in the oil-and-gas department. "Well, we need another clerk in risk arbitrage," he said, "but I can't hire you away from Mr. Dickson. The only way you're going to get out of that department is to go see Cy Lewis."

Cy Lewis? Not encouraging news. Salim L. Lewis—Cy to his familiars—had come to Bear Stearns as a bond salesman in 1932, after having been fired by Salomon Brothers and another firm. He'd been hired by Ted Low, the chief operating partner, who himself had been recruited four years earlier by the founding partners, Joseph Bear, Robert B. Stearns, and Harold C. Mayer—a well-bred, well-heeled triumvirate. When they had opened for business in 1923, Bear was forty-five, ten years older than Stearns and seventeen older than Mayer. He'd been educated in France, Germany, and Switzerland, headed for Wall Street, married money, and eventually became a partner at J. J. Danzig, a small bond-trading firm. After graduating from Yale, Stearns, whose father founded Stern's Department Stores, had gone abroad to study banking, returned home, and joined Danzig as a statistician. Mayer, whom everyone called Bill, was a fellow Midwesterner and he and I would soon develop an easy rapport. He came from Lincoln, Nebraska, where his family, like Stearns's and mine, had prospered in the retail business. He had an Ivy League business degree but (unlike Stearns, frankly) not a whit of pretentiousness. In his early twenties he had started his own export-import business, and when he teamed up with Bear and Stearns he conveniently already owned a seat on the New York Stock Exchange, a $97,000 acquisition financed mostly by his father.

Among the things that set Cy Lewis apart, in addition to being self-made, was that few people mistook him for a gentleman. He dressed well but was approximately as even-tempered and territorial as a grizzly. He skipped college but played minor league professional football, and he looked it— six-four, two hundred forty pounds, and that was before he got heavy. He was smart as hell and long on charisma, a born salesman who knew how to simultaneously charm, amuse, wheedle, and intimidate. As a Jew he assumed, probably correctly, that a lot of the Wall Street Old Guard resented him, and he had no compunction about resenting them. In many respects, it was Cy who had made Bear Stearns a force to be reckoned with. Previously, it had been a small-commission firm whose survival strategy was predicated upon a very low tolerance for risk. All of that changed, however, because Cy had the vision and nerve to go into risk arbitrage and was able to sell the idea to Ted Low and Bill Mayer. (In doing so, he more or less frightened away Stearns, who abruptly decided to retire and become a limited partner.) There's no question that opening up a risk arbitrage department provided an enormous long-term benefit for the likes of me and other young people who joined Bear Stearns. It gave us a chance to trade and to shine.

The lengths Cy went to to cultivate clients could be equally cunning and cringe-inducing. That trade of a million shares of Investor Diversified Services had an emblematic backstory. For years Cy had observed Robert Young from afar, coveting him as a client but unsure how to reel him in. He knew that Young was an avid golfer who frequently played at The Greenbrier, in West Virginia, and he somehow learned when Young was planning to show up for one of his extended visits. Cy got there a few days in advance, found the top pro, and hired him to play a round every day for two weeks. One afternoon the pro announced that he wasn't free the next day because Young was arriving and would expect him to be available. "Oh, no," Cy said. "You and I have a contract. But if you insist, Mr. Young is certainly welcome to play with us." Young had no objection and, naturally, by the end of eighteen holes each had a new friend.

Cy had been at Bear Stearns only a few years when his trading talents and assertiveness made it plain that he would soon be running the firm. His reputation for bluntness and tactlessness made me less than eager to approach him with my hat in my hand. Each morning, he, Low, Mayer, and Bear rode downtown together in Mayer's car. I expected that if I showed up at Cy's office door he would recognize me because for a couple of months I'd made a point of arriving for work before everyone else. When the bosses got off the elevator, they could see me, the earliest bird, talking to the receptionist. This was, believe me, a *very* calculated attempt to demonstrate my intention to work my way up the ladder sooner rather than later.

After Slade told me that I needed to plead my case with Cy, it took me a couple of days to summon the courage. When I finally did—anticlimax. "He isn't in today," his secretary said. "He's playing golf." Would he be in tomorrow? "Yes." So I would have to go through that all over again. Great. Finally, I got past the door, explained that I really wanted to work in risk arbitrage, and that Slade had agreed. "The problem is," I said, "Mr. Dickson thinks I have a great future in the oil department putting pins on maps." Luckily, Cy did not agree. "Don't worry," he said. "I'll take care of it. It's done." And he did and it was.

My first day in that job was inauspicious. Before lunch, Ted Low passed by and said, "You don't look too good. What's the problem?" He motioned for me to follow him into the part-ners' bathroom, where I promptly threw up.

"Mr. Slade is giving me too much to do too fast," I ex-plained. "I'm supposed to be writing down all the trades he's making"—Slade was betting big chunks of the firm's money— "but I can't keep up. I have no idea what I'm doing."

In retrospect, I concede that this was an occasion—but the *only* occasion, with a substantial interval since my fourth-grade run-in with my mother about knickers—when I did in fact freak out on the job. Low put his arm on my shoulder, es-corted me back to Slade, and suggested he ease up. Within a few days, I had grasped the rhythm of the risk arbitrage desk and I was more than happy.

WHEN I was hired by Bear Stearns I had moved to a build-ing at 77th Street and Broadway that was owned by Herman Sarno, the brother of Jay, my college social guru. It turned out to be a total whorehouse. How did I figure that out? I went on a date with one of the other tenants. I had no clue I was supposed to pay her. We didn't have any more dates after that. When Mr. Dickson found out where I was living, he said, "You've got to get out of that place right now." So I moved to a more respectable address, a brownstone in Murray Hill, off Park Avenue in the thirties. My parents came to town and wanted to see where I lived, but I wouldn't let them. I was on the fourth floor, which had six rooms and one bathroom. The neighbors were West Indians who had a habit of singing and dancing all night. Complaining wouldn't have gotten me very far because there were five of them and one of me. I stayed there until one day, on the street, I ran into a friend of mine from Oklahoma City who was visiting another friend of his, Al Davis. I needed a housing arrangement that would make the couple of thousand bucks remaining in my bank account last as long as possible. Al worked in the garment district, was looking for a roommate, and knew a guy in our same situation who worked in public relations, so we rented a basement apartment. We roomed together for two years and the whole time those guys kept trying to trade up. I told them, "Okay, but I'm not doing any looking. Just tell me where to move my trunk." Domestic details were a low priority. I had come to New York with a grander plan.

MOST OF the risk arbitrage in those days derived from bank-ruptcy reorganizations of railroads and utilities that had been ongoing since the 1930s. This was an area of the business that hadn't existed until Cy joined the firm. He became an ob-sessive student of the decline of the railroads, was convinced that the industry was bound to consolidate rather than disap-pear, and in 1934 hired a like-minded sidekick, David Finkle. Superficially, they made an incongruous pair. Davey was a foot shorter than Cy and looked and sounded as if his favorite pastime was watching Jimmy Cagney movies. One of his running gags was to announce loudly that he was leaving for the day and head for the door wearing Cy's cashmere topcoat, which reached his ankles, and Cy's felt homburg, which rested over Davey's ears. What they had most in common was a talent for moving the merchandise. Both were terrific salesmen with energy to match. They cultivated lasting relationships with the chief financial officers of banks, insurance companies, and investment trusts all over the country, selling both bonds and equities, and the size of the trades they executed steadily increased.

Their risk arbitrage strategy involved buying securities that were technically defunct, on the assumption that the assets of the original issuer would emerge from bankruptcy in a viable form. One that had come into play a few months into my apprenticeship was United Light and Railway, a public utility holding company in Kansas City that had gone bust. We bought United Light's preferred stock, betting that a court-approved reorganization plan would entitle us to exchange the preferred for shares of five subsidiary entities, all of which, in theory, had plenty of upside potential. After the plan went through, we sold our new stock on the open market.

I'd then been at Bear Stearns long enough to gain sufficient confidence to call my father and ask to borrow $10,000. I told him about United Light and said, "I think I can make money in the stock market." He was willing but said he'd have to borrow it himself from the bank. Six months later I'd doubled the money and paid him back, plus interest. If I could do that for own account, why couldn't I do it for clients? I'd already qualified for my broker's license. Now I got busy hustling business.

At a cocktail party I met a fellow named Leo Farland, who

worked for Leval & Co., the New York branch of Louis Dreyfus & Cie., one of the largest agricultural commodities deal-
ers in Europe. His office was two blocks from mine and we
started having lunch occasionally. Farland introduced me to
a friend of his named Marcel Aubry, I started doing business
with him, and that led me to Fernand Leval, the head of the
company. Leval was a Swiss émigré, a big man, very gruff, but
he took a liking to me and was happy to take my calls. All
of his trades were for his personal account, starting with a
few hundred shares, which he then ratcheted up to five- or
ten-thousand-share lots. The surest way to earn Aubry's and
Leval's trust was the simplest, by being honest and sincere
and recognizing that if I made a mistake, reacting defensively
would only make it worse. My working vocabulary had to in-
clude the phrase "I was wrong"—an indispensable rule that I
later tried to impress upon our salesmen and traders at Bear
Stearns.

If I wanted more responsibility and stature, I had to demonstrate that I'd been paying attention to big-picture matters
as well as easy-to-overlook details. Very often, the debt securities that Bear Stearns offered to institutional accounts were
obscure issues that the buyers had no idea existed. Which
was how my pleasure reading shifted to spine-tingling thrill-
ers disguised as monthly reports from a U.S. agency called
the Foreign Bondholders Protective Council. Perusing it one
morning I came across a sleeper. In the late 1940s Japan had
agreed to repay all its war debts, plus interest, within ten
years. Among the scores of industrial firms that qualified was
the Shin-Etsu Chemical Company, which had floated bonds
before the war. To ensure that they could meet principal and
interest payments, all the Japanese bond issuers had sinking
funds. Those funds had been dormant during the war but

were now operational. The Foreign Bondholders' report listed the size of each issue that participated in the moratorium and, because there had been a considerable amount of counterfeiting, itemized which ones were still redeemable. This winnowing reduced the outstanding value of certain bond issues, so that some were relatively small compared to their sinking funds. In the case of Shin-Etsu, I could see that bonds then selling at sixty dollars (i.e., 40 percent below par) were going to be retired at par in two years rather than ten. I rushed to show this to Cy and John Slade, who seemed as excited as I was. Our traders got excited, too, and immediately bought as many bonds as they could—which, because the issue was so small, only came to a few hundred thousand dollars' worth. But no matter—my detective work made a distinct impression with my bosses. And they left the distinct impression that they liked what they saw.

Meanwhile, if one of my goals was to enhance my personal bottom line, I'd need to corral more clients. All those years playing football now yielded an unanticipated benefit. My line of attack boiled down to straightforward, three-yards-and-a-cloud-of-dust cold-calling. I loved the challenge. If I came across a name that seemed promising—maybe I knew a friend of his, whatever straw I could hold on to—I'd call the person and say I'd like to come see him. I had to be in the trading room every day from 8:00 a.m. to 6:00 p.m., which limited cold-calling to after hours. I'd heard about a real estate developer named Gus Ring, who lived in Washington and owned a stable of thoroughbreds that he used to race in New York. When I phoned him, he listened to my proposal, bought some bonds, and for all I knew promptly forgot my name. To reel him in as a steady client I needed to meet him in person, which proved more problematical. I'd been told that when he was in New York he spent his days at the track and his nights at the St. Regis Hotel. Every day after work I'd camp out for an hour in the hotel lobby, waiting for him to return from Aqueduct race track, a ruse that I hoped to parlay into a not-so-chance encounter. That never panned out, but Gus eventually became an important account anyway. More than twenty-five years later, when the firm was in a squeeze because Cy Lewis and Ted Low had died and their estates had withdrawn their capital, we decided to bring in a few limited partners, and Gus was the first person we asked. (Among the people we also approached was former Senator Edward Brooke of Massachusetts, who had lost his seat in the previous election. When I made the offer to Brooke, he said he was interested but didn't have a lot of cash to spare. "Can you come up with $5,000?" I asked, and he said he could. This turned out to be a very lucrative investment for him, but that didn't stop him from calling me a couple of years later to tell me he was moving his account from Bear Stearns to a discount broker because they charged lower commissions. As they say in Oklahoma: Oy vey.) Thanks to Gus's cachet, many others followed, and after word got around about our profitability, we were swamped with eager would-be investors. Over the years Gus and I grew to be great pals. He was someone whose friendship and judgment I treasured, and when he died in 1983, I was very touched to be asked to deliver his eulogy. And it had all started from a cold call.

Not long after my little coup with the Shin-Etsu Chemical bonds, another opportunity came along, the Missouri Pacific Railroad's emergence from bankruptcy reorganization. Essentially, risk arbitrage was a matter of making educated bets, but the risk factors differed somewhat from garden-variety stock and bond trading. A tender offer would be handicapped differently from a takeover or a friendly merger. Some mergers the government challenged on antitrust grounds, others were in doubt because of shareholder resistance. When you had reason to believe the government would lose or the management of the takeover target would capitulate, you bet accordingly.

From the creditors' perspective, the Missouri Pacific reorganization outcome depended upon a case before the U.S. Supreme Court. Once the justices had heard oral arguments I made a point of calling the clerk of the court every Monday at 12:30 p.m.—decisions were announced Monday mornings—and asking the same question: Had the Missouri Pacific decision come in? When it finally did, the clerk read it to me and I realized that it was very favorable to one class of bonds. I ran into the partners' lunchroom with the news and they came running out and started scrambling for all the bonds they could get their hands on. They bought them from, among others, L. F. Rothschild, Josephthal, Abraham, Goldman Sachs. These people were our rivals but they were also supposed to be our allies. Cy had once said of Gus Levy, the chairman of Goldman Sachs, "We're friendly competitors. Cut each other's throats between ten and three and after that have great fun together." In this instance, they took serious umbrage at our actions and asked us to cancel all of the trades, which we did. So that one both had and had not worked out as hoped. Still, from my perspective, let's just say, it was a definite win.

CHAPTER

4

In 1948, JOHN SLADE TOOK A HOLIDAY
from the risk arbitrage desk and went to London as a member
of the American delegation to the Summer Olympic games.
The men's field hockey team—Slade played goalie—returned
home without a medal, which usually happens when you lose
all your matches. But there was a tangible reward, an Olympic
blazer, and Slade proudly wore it (for all I know, he showered
and slept in it) throughout his travels right after the Games, a
self-guided tour of European banks during which he would
arrive unannounced and introduce himself as a representative of Bear Stearns.

Before becoming John Slade he had been Hans Schlesinger,
an ambitious young German looking forward to a banking career in Berlin or Frankfurt or Geneva—until the day when
he heard on the radio: "Any Jew caught kissing a gentile girl
will be put in jail." He knew instantly that he would have to
emigrate, and in 1936 he sailed for New York, where he soon
found work at Bear Stearns as a runner—someone who car-
ries messages or securities from one firm to another—for fifteen dollars a week. At the urging of Ted Low (né Lowenstein,
and not the most comfortable-in-his-own-skin Jew I ever
met), he immediately changed his name.

Twelve years later, during his cold-calling expedition, the

Olympic blazer turned out to have limited short-term value; it usually got him in the door and not much further. Still, he knew what he was doing. In Geneva, he went to one bank and placed an order to buy 1,000 shares of the Royal Dutch Company, followed by a stroll into another bank, where he placed a sell order for 1,000 shares. The commissions came to fifty bucks, seed capital in effect. Technically, Bear Stearns now had "done business" with two Swiss banks, and—insert leap of imagination—the Bear Stearns foreign department began to gestate, if just barely.

Back home, Slade grew restless. Railroad and utilities reorganizations had mostly run their course, and merger activity in general declined to about one deal a month. His early vision of a foreign department wasn't elaborate. It amounted to cultivating relationships with European banks and encouraging them to buy securities in American companies, with Bear Stearns in the role of broker. He wanted to see where it would lead. He'd had enough of risk arbitrage and was eager for a literal change of scenery.

No one solicited my opinion, but I let it be known that if John had other priorities, I considered myself available to run risk arbitrage. Putting me in charge at that low-ebb moment, in my view, was no more hazardous than handing me the keys to a hotdog stand. Slade didn't object and neither did Cy or any of the other senior partners, so in the spring of 1953 I took over.

For a change, my timing couldn't have been much better. The stock market was about to commence an eight-year bull run—who knew?—the most sustained in its history. The economy warmed up, companies became more aggressive about buying other companies, and risk arbitrage kept getting livelier and more lucrative.

Some arbitrageurs preferred trying to get a fix on newly launched mergers or tenders by talking to disinterested lawyers. (One who claimed to do that, many years later, was Ivan Boesky, who used to brag that he had a team of accountants and lawyers analyzing every new deal. The reality was that virtually all the decisions he made with professional guidance were losers. His big winners came about because he was paying bankers and lawyers for inside information.)

My approach from the get-go was to study a deal logically and decide what I thought was going to happen. That seemed to work quite well. Whenever I got wind of one, I'd promptly call the chief financial officer of the acquiring company and ask how quickly we could get a look at the proxy material—never insider information, just publicly available stuff. In those early days, our "research department" wasn't of much help to me. It was a one-man operation, a guy named Dave Levy. You'd ask him a question and he'd give you an answer that was supposed to mean something. How could one man know about eight thousand companies? He couldn't. The management thinking behind that approach had been summed up by Cy Lewis: "In an up market I don't need any research, and in a down market a research department will break you." Given the circumstances, it would be accurate to describe my methodology as seat-of-the-pants.

My father used to say about the retail business, "If you don't lose money on accounts receivable, you're cutting off people who are potential clients." Same with risk arbitrage—you can't behave so cautiously that you're not really in the game. You have to get involved in lots of deals. You hope they're all winners, but if you're not losing money on some, it means you're not taking chances, you're not working hard enough.

No one questioned my work ethic. By then I was living in

the same apartment building as John Rosenwald, who had come to Bear Stearns in 1954. Johnny would become one of my closest friends, also one of the most successful salesmen in the firm's history. We'd ride to work together and often commiserate about, among other things, the compensation system. Basically, you received your salary and a bonus five times that. The partners told you what you were getting, and if you were unhappy they said, "Wait until next year." That first full year running risk arbitrage my bonus came to $35,000, which sounds great for 1954 but only if you ignore that it was dwarfed by my contribution to the bottom line. I went to Davey Finkle and I was burning. This was the same year Notre Dame had hired Terry Brennan, a twenty-five-year-old, as its football coach. Davey asked me how old I was, which I found patronizing. I told him, "I'm two years older than the head coach at Notre Dame!" He broke out laughing and said, "You're too quick for me." And that was the end of our meeting. For the moment, nothing had changed, but long-term, I suspected, my leverage would improve.

Soon enough, I was taking home $100,000 a year. I liked the sound of that; it compared favorably with what Ted Williams was getting. Then I hit a speed bump. It wasn't unusual for certain clients to become fixtures, more or less, in our trading rooms. They would show up almost every weekday and occupy desk space near our account representatives, who would execute their trades. Not knowing better, you might assume that they were employees. (We were still a generation away from the middle-class's transformation from scrupulous savers to credit-hungry consumers and risk-happy investors. Even further from the advent of online discount brokerages and the popular delusion that anyone with a computer, a hunch, and a thousand dollars could plunge right in and beat the market. But I digress.) Among the regulars in the trading room was an interesting character named Johannes Steel, a newspaper columnist and radio commentator who specialized in politics and economics, with a left-wing bias. He compiled an erratic record as a prognosticator: he predicted the attack on Pearl Harbor a week before it happened and, near the end of his life, the market crash of October 1987. But he was too optimistic by several years in prophesying Hitler's demise.

I no longer recall the exact claims Steel made about one particular Alaskan gold mining company he was promoting. (And I wish I'd prophesied that many years down the road, in an entirely different matter, he'd be convicted of stock fraud.) His pitch to me and five other account representatives was that if we helped him sell the stock he'd give us options. All of us felt comfortable enough that I ended up selling shares to my father and his brothers and Gus Ring, and I bought some for myself. Nothing was done in secrecy. Steel was almost a part of the firm in our minds, and it didn't occur to us that we were doing anything we shouldn't.

Unfortunately, in the process we'd broken a New York Stock Exchange rule that said that any consideration received by an employee in the course of executing a securities transaction had to go directly to the firm. If Bear Stearns had received the options and passed them to us, that would have been kosher. Instead, we were all found guilty of a technical violation and suspended for two months. I spent most of this unplanned vacation in Oklahoma City, pleasantly surprising my dear mom, who had claimed that I'd never come home again, you may recall. If my misstep caused unhappiness among the elders at Bear Stearns, no one ever mentioned it. I'm inclined to think it didn't. Less than two years later—in 1958, the year I turned thirty-one—I was made a partner.

As I discovered the nuances of risk arbitrage, one of my most helpful mentors was Bernard J. (Bunny) Lasker, a pragmatic and levelheaded arbitrageur (and future chairman of the New York Stock Exchange). Bunny and I met at a golf club we both belonged to and immediately became friends; the fact that he was twice my age was neither here nor there. Soon we were having regular get-togethers at the Stock Exchange luncheon club. He'd ask, "What do you like?" I'd tell him and he'd say, "Okay, buy me ten thousand"—or whatever. And we charged a big commission. Bunny was doing this with a lot of brokers—buying stocks that sounded good but not necessarily holding them for long. His standing instructions were: "If it goes up a point, buy me more. If it goes up another point, call me. If it goes down two points, sell it."

This sane, simple advice—unload losers, ride winners—became a source of enduring mystery for me: Why didn't more investors embrace it? And why did so many, Cy Lewis included, do just the opposite?

Cy's strengths were the flip side of his weaknesses. What defined him as a salesman and trader—his bravado and self-confidence—came from having compiled a mostly winning record. But he had a self-subverting unwillingness to take losses. During his prime, which extended from the mid-thirties to the mid-sixties, Bear Stearns had three main sources of income: institutional trading, arbitrage, and trading for the firm's own account. Along with Gus Levy at Goldman Sachs, Cy had pioneered the block trading of common stocks with institutions. If we held, say, 10,000 shares of Company X in our own account, the stock could be resold on the market over time, in small lots. Or it could be traded as a block—the whole kaboodle in a single transaction. Block trading required the partners of Bear Stearns to expose their capital to large positions in individual stocks that they might not have even heard of before the client called and wanted a bid. Cy felt that any block he bought was destined to go up simply because he owned it. You can imagine how accurate that was. Fractional fluctuations in price could yield swift and substantial profits. But this was a double-edged, high-adrenaline game that could easily lead to hubris and a dangerous faith in the infallibility of one's hunches. We were buying a position from an institution that had researched the stock—often a company we didn't even know the ticker symbol of before they called—and decided they wanted out. We were, to put it mildly, on the wrong side of the vigorish. More about that later.

In 1954 Bob Stearns died, as did Joe Bear the following year, and the year after that Davey Finkle retired. Whereupon John Slade came to me with a request that I wanted nothing more than to refuse. Would I be willing to assume Davey's seat at the trading desk—meaning, would I agree to become Cy's assistant? A recipe for instant *agita?*—no thanks. Stylistically and philosophically, Cy and I had very little in common. I hadn't yet become a partner—that would happen in 1958—but I approached my responsibilities as if I were. The well-being of the firm had to take precedence over diplomatic niceties. From a distance Cy and I could coexist peacefully enough, I believed. What I was being asked to do, however, would change the game entirely. Slade understood my reasons, but in his mind they were trumped by the exigencies of the moment—and the future. "Only you can take that seat," he said, "because it will hold Cy's successor."

The odd thing was that Cy had no illusions about the differences in our temperaments. "Alan treats securities like toilet paper," he would say years later, referring to my willingness to sell any security—*any*—if I didn't like how it was behaving. Fine with me. Nor did I mind when he also told a reporter, "Alan is a better trader than I'll ever be. If he owns a stock and it goes down, it trades. I don't care if his mother's the president of the company, out it goes—there's no sentimentality connected to it all." This statement showed that Cy actually could see himself objectively at moments, but it didn't mean that he could muster the self-discipline to alter his habits.

My own discipline derived from another of my father's retail maxims: "If something isn't moving, sell it today because tomorrow it's going to be worth less." I'd come to understand—something Bunny and I often discussed—that nobody really knows what's going on inside any company, including the president. They only think they know. When a stock starts acting badly relative to the market, it's either an anomaly or a sign that something's really wrong. Whichever, it's time to get out. I'm not talking about when the entire market is trending down but when it's going well. If whatever's happening with the specific stock is indeed an anomaly, you can always buy it back. In my experience there's very little to be said for dollar-averaging—continuing to buy a stock as it drops because you keep lowering your average per-share basis. I say this with one caveat: if your goal is to be the largest shareholder when the company goes into bankruptcy, then it's a great system.

In Cy's mind, it seemed, if he bought a stock it could do

no wrong. (If it headed south, it became irrelevant, ignored, forgotten—yet remained on the books.) This certitude struck me as perverse and arrogant. What offended me above all was Cy's indifference to the best interests of the partnership. And it placed us on an unavoidable collision course. By 1960, when I'd been at Bear Stearns for eleven years and a partner for two, I owned about 3 percent of the equity. We were still profitable, despite Cy's habit of riding losses.

In the spring of 1962, President Kennedy had successfully outmaneuvered the major American steel manufacturers, causing them to roll back a planned increase in steel prices. It was a time, in general, of economic anxiety and fears of inflation. Corporate America had become so preoccupied with suspicions of further government intrusion that the stock market went into a steep downturn. Situations like this never did much to lift my spirits, and this one coincided with a deeper unease I was feeling, a visceral reaction to Cy's willful obtuseness. When I looked at our books and pondered some of the dogs that we'd continued to hold for no good reason, I would feel physically ill. Finally, I walked into Cy's office one afternoon and announced that I was quitting.

"You can't quit," he said.

"Of course I can," I said.

"Why do you want to do this?"

"There's no point in discussing it," I said. "You wouldn't understand."

"No, you have to explain why," he insisted. "You've got to come to my house and talk this over. You owe me that. To-night."

So I went to his house, a huge apartment at 73rd and Park, eighteen rooms, seven bathrooms. I knew it well because I often played bridge there on weekends. Cy was alone, except for his butler. We sat in the library. There were no preliminaries.

"Okay. Again. Why do you want to quit?"

"Have you ever heard of Rudd-Melikian?" I asked.

"No, what the hell is that?"

"It's a stock. You bought it. We own ten thousand shares of it. It's gone from twenty to five. We have *at least twenty positions* like that. I can't stand it another day."

He sat there silently for a while, then said, "Look, I know, I have trouble selling things."

I was still waiting to hear something I didn't already know. Finally, he got around to it. "Okay, Alan, I'll make you a deal. From now on, you're free to sell anything you want that has a loss in it. You hear me? Anything that has a loss. And I also promise that I'll do my best to live with it. Agreed?"

"Agreed."

When I got to the office the next day, Cy wasn't yet there. I called Moe Baker, the head of the order room, and told him, "Get a pencil and paper. I want to give you some sell orders." I picked up the position book and said, "Sell ten thousand Rudd-Melikian; sell twenty thousand XYZ, ten thousand this, that, whatever." I noticed that everyone around me had stopped talking and was looking at me. They couldn't believe what they were seeing and hearing. The market opened in a few minutes. Moe went to the phone and called Bill Mayer, our head broker on the floor of the Exchange. Bill—a wonderful guy, I loved him—was one of the founders of Bear Stearns and held the largest amount of capital of any of the partners. But like everyone else, he had no desire to cross Cy. He sees these orders coming through and wants to know where they came from. Moe tells him they're from me. So Bill went to an outside phone, called me, and said, "Are you trying to get yourself killed?"

I said, "It's okay, I had a meeting with Cy last night and we're not riding losses anymore. We're selling them. And this is the start."

"You really know what you're doing?"

I assured him that I did. The next question was what to do with the money. At the time there was a big merger pending—American Viscose, a chemical business, was trying to be bought, but the government was holding it up on anti-trust grounds. I thought the deal would eventually go through and I wasn't alone. I told Bill that I wanted to put most of the proceeds from the losers we'd just unloaded into American Viscose. The spread looked good. And Joe Gruss, one of the biggest speculators on Wall Street, was so confident he was telling everyone to buy American Viscose because "they're the same thing as Jewish treasury bills."

As we were putting through that order, I said to Bill, "If this merger doesn't go through, you're on your way home to Nebraska and I'll be shipped back to Oklahoma." I had this brief vision of everything I'd just sold going up and American Viscose straight down. Instead, six weeks later the merger was approved.

That one incident made my career and, I think, made Bear Stearns. Many years later, at moments when I wanted to guide us strategically in new directions—greatly expand our retail sales network or establish a large-scale clearing business—Cy did not get in my way.

Cy could never circumvent our agreement, as far as I was concerned. To try to help him see it in a broader context, I proposed the creation of a risk committee that would evaluate the potential downside of acquiring or maintaining large holdings in specific stocks and would track how the firm's capital was invested in various market sectors. Its membership consisted of myself, a couple of other partners, and Cy, who had so little patience with the process that the committee soon disbanded. However, my authority to sell any securities that we had losses in remained in place. There were occasions when Cy tried to wish it away, but I never relented, and why would I? My track record provided the credibility I needed. When we had the market going our way, the risk arbitrage department accounted for 50 percent of the firm's profits, and in a slow year it accounted for 100 percent. Still, as long as Cy continued to trade, we inevitably threw a tremendous amount of money out the window every year. So he and I had our periodic dust-ups.

For instance, there was the 100,000-share block of AT&T that he bought from Steve Ross, of Warner Communications. The stock started going down and I told Cy I was selling it. This triggered the familiar backsliding.

"You can't sell *that*," he said.

"Why not?"

"It's Telephone. You don't sell Telephone"—meaning, evidently, that it was synonymous with God and motherhood.

I said, "Cy, it's a stock. Any stock can go down, no matter what it is."

No, he insisted, this was different. "Just a minute," he said. "We've gotta bring in somebody else." In the trading room I sat to Cy's left, Johnny Rosenwald was on his right. For private conversations, his glass-walled office was nearby.

"Look, Johnny," Cy said after we'd closed the door. "I've

bought this block of stock. AT&T. I think it's going up. If I'm right it'll make you and all the other young partners a lot of money."

And Johnny said, "But, Cy, if it goes down any more it'll *cost* the young partners a lot of money."

I thought Cy was going to fall off his chair. We left the office, I started selling the stock, and in fact it did keep going down. A couple of years later, it came back, but why would we want to tie up so much capital waiting for that to happen?

So the routine became that if I sold something Cy had bought he wouldn't say anything, but if a stock recovered he would frequently punch it into his Quotron machine and it would appear on the overhead electronic ticker as a periodic reminder to all. One day when he was at lunch I went to his machine, cleared it of all the stocks he'd been following, and put on there every stock I'd sold in the previous twelve months that hadn't recovered. He came back and said, "What's this?" I said, "Well, Cy, I thought you might want to see some of the things you bought that didn't do so well." So much for that bit of guerrilla warfare.

The most dramatic of our altercations took place a couple of years after the meeting at Cy's apartment. This time he'd bought a block of convertible bonds issued by the Celanese Corporation. One Friday morning I saw that the bonds had weakened and decided to sell them. Cy trotted out some inventive logic.

"What are you doing?" he said. "You can't sell those. They're bonds."

"Cy, bonds can go down in price, too. We're selling." (In 2008, of course, we would find out just how rapidly and ruinously bonds could go down.)

"If you're selling, I'll buy 'em," he said.

"Okay. How many do you want? $100,000 worth?" I turned to my assistant on the trading desk, Marvin Davidson. "Marvin, make out a ticket. You just sold $100,000 Celanese bonds to Cy." Marvin looked terrified. "You want more, Cy?"

"Yeah, I'll take another hundred."

"Marvin, make out another ticket . . . Still want some more?"

He bought another hundred and as he headed for the door, in a rush to get to his weekend place in New Jersey, said to me, "I'll see *you* in my office Monday morning!" I continued selling the bonds.

The following Monday I came in early, ready to kick his ass. I wanted to kill him. Which would have been improbable because he outweighed me by at least a hundred pounds. Not that it was necessary. Before I could get out a word, Cy said, "I was wrong. You were right. I'm sorry. Let's get back to work."

Which I proceeded to do, having again confirmed what had been clear since our showdown in his apartment. Nominally, Cy might remain the head of the firm, but we'd come to a defining moment in my life and in the history of Bear Stearns. My veto over his trading habits signified unmistakably that I had taken over. We both knew it and so did everyone who worked there. For the next forty years, that was how things would be.

5

Experience, according to the pro-verbial wisdom, is a great teacher. Also, we should learn from our mistakes. Or, if you prefer: good judgment comes from experience, and experience comes from bad judgment. Et cetera.

Without disputing these truisms, I have to say that I'd just as soon avoid the trial-and-error enlightenment that dawns during the mop-up after one's own stupidities. I'd much rather glean lasting understanding from the blunders of others—far less wear and tear. Paradoxically, or maybe not, most of my education in how to motivate and manage people and how to lead by example was the byproduct of lessons learned, directly or indirectly, by observing two people— my father and Cy Lewis, who shared few if any personality or character traits—as they responded sensibly, or not, to adversity.

Case in point: My father, I always felt, was greatly disad-vantaged by his loyalty to his brothers. Please don't misun-derstand; nothing matters more to me than family—my wife and her family, my children and grandchildren, siblings and their spouses and offspring, multiple generations of cousins. Which is why I want to be on good terms with all of them.

And why I'm careful to avoid whatever might jeopardize those relationships. As I've mentioned, my father was the youngest of six brothers as well as, atypically, the boss of the family business. Watching him cope with various shortcomings of his brothers, individuals who I truly cared for but knew too much about to revere, convinced me that I never wanted to work in that sort of business. From an early age, I heard more than I wanted to about which of my uncles wasn't pulling his weight and with what consequences. It was as if I had a front-row seat on an unwritten elaboration of Parkinson's Law: the larger the number of family members employed by the same enterprise, the greater the opportunity for resentment, thus negating the benefit of employing large numbers of family members in the first place.

So, in 1960, when a situation arose that most people would deem quite awkward, I didn't waste time pondering what to do. My assistant on the risk arbitrage desk was Eddie Hirsch, a bright, alert, and highly capable guy who one day surprised me with the news that he'd become engaged to my sister, DiAnne. I knew at once that I had to fire him. He'd done nothing wrong and I didn't intend to either. Shortly before the wedding, his mother confronted me in a rage. "How could you do that?" she demanded. I explained that I simply wasn't going to work with my brother-in-law, just as I wasn't going to work with my kids when they got to be old enough. Bear Stearns didn't then have a formal nepotism policy, but I did.

In 1971 I realized that we twenty-five partners, myself included, had among us thirty children aged ten to fifteen. The clear implication—to me, anyway—was that the moment had arrived to draft such a policy. This memorandum was directed not only at partners; it meant we will not hire anybody related to anybody in the firm. We wanted to keep the entire orga-nization clean of family. I expected resistance but met with surprisingly little.

Ted Low, whom no one ever accused of being a visionary, said, "If we do what you're proposing, we're going to lose a lot of bright people."

"I'm sure you're right about that," I told him. "And if we don't do it, we're going to hire a hundred percent of the dummies."

That settled the debate. The policy, as adopted, couldn't have been less ambiguous. It defined family as "brother, sister, father, mother, son, daughter, son-in-law, daughter-in-law, brother-in-law, sister-in-law, aunt, uncle, niece, nephew, grandchild." A couple of years later, Cy invited Johnny Rosen-wald and me into his office and announced that he had "great news." Which was? "I want to bring my son into the business." Cy had three sons and one daughter, and the son he had in mind was his eldest, Sandy. Johnny and I didn't even look at each other. We both knew that this was anything but great news.

"Cy, we can't do that," I said. "We have a rule."

"Rules can be broken on certain occasions," he insisted.

"But this rule is working beautifully. We cannot start taking sons, sons-in-law, daughters into the firm. That's just the way it is. Sandy is very capable and he'll have no trouble getting another job."

We left it at that. Until a week later, when a Bear Stearns partner named Mark Stewart Sr. came to see me. "You've got to do something for Cy's son," he said.

"Mark, we're not going to take in children of partners, in-cluding Cy's son."

"It's important to Cy."

"It's very important to me that we *don't* do it."

As LONG as Cy remained the titular head of Bear Stearns, skirmishes of this sort would occasionally arise. I never enjoyed them and I tried hard to be deferential because gratuitous antagonism would have benefited no one. Besides, after our watershed confrontation in his apartment many years earlier I'd never doubted my leverage or my logic. If the firm was going to thrive the culture had to evolve, and it wouldn't happen as a result of conflict and conquest. It would have to emerge from cumulative judgments about what constituted worthwhile risks and opportunities.

There was zero chance that we would plot our future by superimposing any grandiose blueprint or manifesto upon Bear Stearns as we then knew it. I'm notorious for my antipathy to long-range planning, reliance upon outside consultants, and euphemistic corporate-speak. My strategic thinking boiled down to a conviction that whatever boosted morale and camaraderie should also help boost profits. Common sense, self-assurance, and controlling costs would guide us through up markets, down markets, auspicious circumstances, and the opposite. And every year a handful of partners would determine the bonuses for nonpartners, an outcome that had to be based upon merit and a credible standard of fairness. I made certain that it got a *lot* fairer on my watch, as Johnny Rosenwald and I, during our low-on-the-totem-pole years, had vowed it would. To do otherwise would have been self-defeating. I'd watched how my father conducted himself with the employees at Street's, many of whom spent their entire lives with that company. They'd been shown respect and had reciprocated with affection for and loyalty to the owners. At Bear Stearns I'd experienced firsthand the arrogance of some senior people toward low-level employees. Cy's commentary about my complete lack of sentimentality as a trader served me well because it was consistent with my style as a manager. But no matter what ambitions I harbored, I was determined never to leave cleat marks on anybody's back. The people I worked with from the beginning would remain my friends throughout my business career. I don't think I ever stepped on anybody.

When I came to Bear Stearns in 1949, the partnership's accumulated capital stood at $18 million, and when I became a partner nine years later it had grown to $30 million. Our annual net profits were retained as capital. Each partner received a relatively modest guaranteed salary—in the mid-'70s, about $60,000 per year after taxes (a figure that by 2007, our last full year in business, had reached $250,000 for senior managing directors)—plus 6 percent interest on one's accumulated capital. Every two years, the compensation committee would recalculate how profit shares would be allocated for the entire partnership, a division of the pie that (in theory) was strictly performance-based. The fact that everyone had so much of his net worth invested in the firm Johnny called a "wonderful form of indentured slavery." We made it quite difficult to take out money. Withdrawals had to be approved by the executive committee, according to stringent criteria: only by leaving the firm—dying being the usual, if not the preferred, method—could a partner fully liquidate his equity. Otherwise, a capital account could be tapped to pay school tuition or to make a down payment on a house but not for routine discretionary spending. A medical emergency might or might not qualify. It was tacitly assumed that if a family member of a partner were kidnapped the committee would almost certainly authorize a withdrawal to pay ransom. Not that the vote would necessarily be unanimous.

My veto agreement with Cy somehow qualified me for the dubious privilege of a slot in his morning carpool. For a while during the mid-fifties I'd ridden downtown every day with Johnny Rosenwald and John Gutfreund, a future CEO of Salomon Brothers who then worked in its municipal bond department. Gutfreund drove a green Oldsmobile convertible, refused to let us chip in for gas or parking, and invoked a simple edict that we were delighted to abide by: no talking. If only that had been the rule in Cy's car. I had moved to the building where I still live, on the East Side, close to Central Park, and Cy would pick me up there at eight o'clock. An institutional salesman named Jerry Goldstein lived a half-block from me and also rode down with us. He and I sat in the front seat with the driver—in those days of bench seats you could fit three people in the front of a car—and Cy rode in back with Ted Low. It was several miles to Wall Street and only on rare mornings did Cy and Ted fail to get into some nonsensical discussion or argument that would have had me tearing my hair out if I'd had any to spare. Jerry used to sit there and giggle. He liked to tell people that by 42nd Street I could have used a drink even though it was eight o'clock in the morning.

The repartee didn't get any better when we arrived at the office. The first time I heard Cy refer to our retail salesmen, who dealt most directly with the public, as "the schmucks out front," I failed to find it funny and told him so. I felt the same way the umpteenth time he did it. It dismayed me to know that our sales reps often heard it, too. (In fairness to Cy, he was an equal-opportunity offender. After his death, in 1978, one of the first things I did was to call and apologize to many people whom I knew he had insulted. I apologized to Morris Shapiro, of M.A. Shapiro & Company, Wall Street's leading banking expert. I apologized to Don Regan, the chief executive of Merrill Lynch. When I called Homer Budge, the chairman of the board of Investors Diversified Services, and began, "I know Cy was insulting . . . ," he said, "You mean when he told me I was too dumb to come in out of the rain? I got used to that.")

A Bear Stearns bond salesman whom I'll call Frank Jones once went to Johnny Rosenwald and said, "I have to leave the firm."

"Why?" John asked.

"Because Cy thinks I'm a jerk."

Johnny told him to take it easy, then came to me, and together we went to see Cy.

"When you don't like someone at the firm you've got to do a better job of concealing your feelings," I said. "People are sensitive about that."

"Who's complaining?" Cy demanded.

"Frank Jones," Johnny said.

"I don't know why he would say that? I treat everyone the same around here. I've always been perfectly friendly. Never had a cross word with him. Of course, he's the dumbest fucking guy I ever met in my life."

The silver lining of Cy's boorishness was that it made it easier for a leader with a collegial approach to enlist a constituency for change. In the mid-sixties, Johnny and I began a push to expand our retail operation. In New York, we had enough space and back-office capability to double our sales force. At the time, our only satellite office was on LaSalle Street in Chicago, a branch we'd acquired inadvertently decades earlier by taking over a failing brokerage firm whose trades we'd been clearing—that is, processing confirmations, settlements, and the transfer of funds from buyer to seller. In the years since, the Chicago office had concentrated on institutional sales and support of our floor traders at the commodities and options exchanges. Now we began adding retail salesmen and other staff, and over the course of a decade or so we opened branches in Boston, Los Angeles, San Francisco, Dallas, and Atlanta. In each case, we started small—only a handful of employees, usually limited to institutional equity sales—and slowly expanded into retail, municipal and corporate bonds, government bonds, and corporate finance. Growth merely for the sake of growing was never our objective, nor were we ever tempted to build a vast retail sales force à la Merrill Lynch or Smith Barney.

Our fundamental shared assumptions were: We would remain a meritocracy; we would promote from within; an employee who saw a job that he or she felt qualified to do could make a case without fear of peremptory rejection. Same with anyone, at any level, who perceived an overlooked business opportunity or a way to cut costs or increase efficiency. Though I was de facto running the firm, there was no chain of command. Anyone with qualms about the status quo, operationally or ethically or otherwise, could bring them to the attention of any senior executive able to make an informed evaluation. If fixing a problem necessitated going around anybody, including me, so be it.

IN THE summer of 1970, a situation arose that, in the minds of many people with a keen interest in the outcome—by which I mean, among others, the officers and governors of the New York Stock Exchange, the Securities and Exchange Commission, the Federal Reserve, the Department of the Treasury, the

White House—posed a risk to the stability of the entire securities industry and, by extension, the economy as a whole. At the time, brokerage firms were closing their doors left and right (chronic mismanagement was a major factor) and, as a consequence, the NYSE's special trust fund, which existed to protect the firms' customers in such situations, was itself on the ropes. The most urgent cause for concern was the de facto insolvency of Hayden, Stone & Company, a venerable firm with an extensive retail branch network and an active underwriting business that desperately needed a merger partner. Investors had been pulling out their capital for over a year. Things had gotten so dire that Hayden, Stone had enlisted a group of Oklahoma corporations—why Oklahoma I never knew—to pledge as replacement capital more than $17 million of their own stock in return for notes with a 7 percent coupon (interest rate). Before long, though, one of the Oklahoma companies, Four Seasons Nursing Centers of America, was itself in bankruptcy (and would go on to distinguish itself, according to federal prosecutors at the time, as the largest criminal securities fraud in history—but that is, truly, another story).

When a viable merger candidate at last emerged—Cogan, Berlind, Weill & Levitt—the final obstacle was getting the approval of Hayden, Stone's subordinated lenders, who were likely to lose most if not all of their money. The only potential satisfaction these creditors had, really, was a perverse fantasy—the likelihood that their refusal to go along would wipe out the NYSE trust fund and place the entire institution in serious jeopardy. One by one, the lenders fell into line until there was a lone holdout, Jack Golsen, whose company, LSB Industries, Inc., was taking a $1.2 million hit. Golsen was furious. "I'm interested in justice being done," he said at the time. "I want an example made. The only way to make it is to go to a liquidation and let the Exchange lose $25 million or so. I want this crime to be brought to the attention of the public."

A deadline was set of 10:00 a.m. on September 11. The night before, while attending a charity dinner, I got a call from Bunny Lasker, my early mentor and old friend, telling me that a guy in Oklahoma City named Jack Golsen was holding all of Wall Street hostage. Did I know him? As a matter of fact, he'd married a girl who lived down the street from me. Bunny was by now the chairman of the Exchange's board of governors and he wanted me to call Jack to see if I could convince him to go along with the proposed deal. If I hadn't gotten involved, Bunny's Hail-Mary fallback was to have President Richard Nixon intervene.

"I understand that you're upset and I understand why," I told Jack that same night. "But if you don't sign this thing you're going to make some important enemies." Then I rattled off the roster, from Bunny to the president of the United States, and said, "Bunny Lasker is an honest man and a good friend of mine, and I want you to do what he wants because I ask you."

The next day, with ten minutes to go before the deadline, Jack signed, the merger was approved, and that brush with the apocalypse passed. I received a telegram from Jack that afternoon that said,

DEAR ALAN YOUR TELEPHONE CALL WAS INSTRUMENTAL IN MY AGREEING TO GO ALONG WITH BUNNY LASKER'S REQUEST THIS MORNING YOU MAY AS WELL GET ALL THE BROWNIE POINTS YOU CAN BECAUSE THAT'S ALL THAT WILL EVER COME OUT OF THE DEAL REGARDS JACK GOLSEN.

From Bunny came a letter that said:

> As Chairman of the Board of the New York Stock Exchange,
> I write formally for our entire industry. The public and the
> financial community of the world are indebted to you for
> your generous, intelligent and tremendous help in facilitat-
> ing the Cogan, Berlind, Hayden Stone merger. As my close
> friend, God bless you. As ever, Bunny.

The story doesn't end there. As long as the financial community of the world was indebted to me, wouldn't it be foolish
not to try to make this gratitude pay off for Bear Stearns? A
high-flying company called Equity Funding Corporation of
America, then trading on the American Stock Exchange, was
about to move over to the Big Board. If Bunny felt like designating us as the specialist firm for this stock, we would have
no objection. Bunny was happy to accommodate. The trading
in Equity Funding turned out to be very active and therefore
very profitable for us, sufficiently for other firms to go crazy
that we'd been given this plum.

Then, in 1973, the whole thing blew up, the result of a
massive fraud that made the Four Seasons scandal look like
a purse-snatching. The stock of Equity Funding went from
$30 to nothing overnight. We were long about 30,000 shares,
which meant we had a loss of $900,000. When you made a
stock trade in 1973, you had to deliver it within five days. I
notified everybody we'd bought stock from and said we'd pay
them but they had to deliver their stock certificates to us.
The NYSE said no, we had to pay now—Bunny had by then
stepped down as chairman of the Exchange—and, if we had
a claim, we could settle it later. We said, "Listen, we'll pay.

We just want to make sure these are authentic stock certificates." Almost all of the stock we'd agreed to buy had come to us from brokers acting on behalf of insiders, who were in fact prohibited from selling. In the end, virtually every broker asked us to cancel the trades and we came out whole.

I learned two lessons: One, if you do a favor for somebody he may or may not remember; and two, if you do a favor for an institution you'd better collect on your quid pro quo immediately because whoever is running the place today might not be around tomorrow.

DURING THOSE same years, in the early seventies, I pushed for a policy that required Bear Stearns partners to donate at least 4 percent of their gross income to charity. They all agreed to comply and we took their word for it. Then, just to make sure—this became known as the Greenberg Honor System—we checked tax returns. The multiple benefits seemed as self-evident as the rationale for cutting losses, keeping a tight rein on expenses, accumulating capital, or nurturing a meritocracy. We'd be collectively engaged in an intrinsically worthwhile endeavor, we'd strengthen our solidarity and enhance our public identity as corporate citizens, we'd be entitled to feel good about ourselves. If the firm had an even better performance the following year, we'd donate more and earn the right to feel even better. Several other Wall Street firms called and inquired about how we did it, but not one ever established a similar philanthropic policy. I could never figure out why; the whole thing made—and never stopped making—perfect business sense.

Along with the ample creature comforts my parents provided as I was growing up, I'd been blessed with their positive example of philanthropy. If that hadn't been part of my upbringing, I would've gotten the message early in my Bear Stearns career. Cy devotedly embraced the 4 percent rule. In 1950, he and Bill Mayer, who were always generous givers, had escorted me to my first United Jewish Appeal (aka Federation of Jewish Philanthropies) dinner, where I made a pledge of a hundred dollars. For whatever reason, I remember that donation more vividly than any of my specific UJA pledges in the years since—which have totaled many millions. What impressed me about Cy, beyond his generosity, was his energy and commitment as a fundraiser. He became president of the Federation of Jewish Philanthropies, he was quite active in the American Red Cross and the Urban Coalition, and he founded and served as president of the Young Men's and Young Women's Hebrew Associations. During the last ten or fifteen years of his life, after ceding management authority to me, he assumed the mantle of Wall Street gray eminence. Philanthropy and volunteerism occupied a great deal of his time. And intermittently—whenever he felt the urge to remind the Street that he was still in the game—he would deliver pronouncements on this or that financial or public policy issue of the day.

These good works, I think, diverted Cy from some challenges that loomed in the not-distant future. By the early seventies, it had become obvious that the days of fixed commissions for stock and bond trading were numbered, a change that almost certainly would (and did) put out of business a large number of firms whose only revenue sources were brokering trades and selling research. Before the transition, the commission for all New York Stock Exchange trades was fixed at so many cents per share, depending upon the price of the stock. Overnight—the new rule went into effect on May 1, 1975 — the average commission dropped by 75 percent. (The concept of online discount brokerages — the 5,000-share trade of, say, IBM, which thirty-five years ago included a $1,500 commission but today can be executed online for $8.95 — was, for the moment, unthinkable.) The effect upon Bear Stearns was that our commissions from block-trading and institutional sales — Cy's specialties and for decades a bread-and-butter revenue stream — shrank drastically and permanently. But even knowing that fixed rates were doomed, as May 1 approached Cy was insisting that the premium we offered to both institutional and retail clients (expertise, service, research) would exempt us from lowering our rates. Gus Levy of Goldman Sachs had the same fantasy. The market dictated a different outcome; on day one we had no choice but to cut our rates by 75 percent, like everyone else. Goldman did likewise. The delusion lasted another forty-eight hours or so at Loeb Rhoades before it hit them why their phones had stopped ringing.

Two years earlier, we'd moved to new offices at 55 Water Street, having outgrown our original quarters at 1 Wall Street. By 1973 we employed six hundred people in New York alone and more than a hundred in the branch offices. The so-called go-go years of the 1960s had given way to recession, inflation, a Dow in a prolonged decline — off 45 percent in 1973 alone — and pervasive gloom. Thanks in part to risk arbitrage but mainly to what were called "special offerings," we had managed to show a small profit that year. In a special offering, we sold at a deep discount equities that we'd just bought at an even deeper discount. Basically, we'd look for stocks that weren't going anywhere — trading at, say, $10 a share and languishing in the inventories of institutions that were embarrassed to have them on their books. We'd take big blocks off their hands for $3 a share and immediately announce on the Dow Jones news tape that we were doing a secondary offering at $3.25. Brokers would rush in—"An unbelievable bargain," they could tell their retail clients, "two days ago it was at $10!"—and we'd rake in terrific profits. Which is how, almost alone among the major Wall Street firms, we managed to finish that year in the black.

THE MOVE to 55 Water Street burdened us with a lot more overhead. We'd swung a sweet deal on our lease, but we'd rented 120,000 square feet more than we needed. Meanwhile, scores of small brokerage houses (i.e., potential subtenants) had folded. To make the surplus space pay for itself, my solution was to go into an entirely new business: clearing. We'd do for other firms what they would just as soon not be bothered with—documenting their trades, sending out confirmations, collecting dividends, handling their margin accounting, taking in and dispensing money—and in the process we'd collect a small fee for every transaction (while enjoying the overnight float on our clients' and their customers' money). Starting out, we'd woo clients by offering them free rent. Ted Low opposed the whole idea, calling it dumb, which was his way of saying he didn't want us dirtying our hands with something this humdrum. He maintained that we should just devote ourselves to doing business with DuPont and General Motors and the like. ("They're taken," I told him.) To me, the steadiness and predictability of clearing transactions constituted its principal appeal. Our clients would be able to rid themselves of a cumbersome necessity and concentrate on what they knew how to do—sell. It took some time to get our shop up and running, but by early 1975 we were in business.

For several years we had no more than a dozen clients, but in time clearing became a reliable cash cow for us. Two of our biggest competitors, A. G. Becker and Loeb, Rhoades, walked away from it in the mid-'80s and most of their clients came to us. By 1988 we were processing 10 percent of all trades on the New York Stock Exchange, and ultimately we did clearing for two thousand firms.

As this new venture prospered, a more lucrative opportunity was unfortunately slipping away. When negotiated rates began, I urged Johnny Rosenwald to shift from institutional sales to corporate finance. His time and energy would be more profitably spent—the reduced commissions for institutional accounts were an incentive killer—and the firm could tap more deeply into his talent for knowing and getting along with, it seemed, everybody. And I had a broader motive, to rejuvenate a corporate finance department that had never really fulfilled its promise.

For starters, the department's co-heads, Sig Wahrsager and Jerome Kohlberg, couldn't stand each other. Sig, who was a confidant of Cy's, had a traditional approach to investment banking: hustling underwritings of new issues and hoping that those relationships could lead to even more rewarding merger-and-acquisition business. He was smart and a deft office politician. Jerry Kohlberg had come to Bear Stearns in 1955, when he was thirty, to work in the research department, and shifted to corporate finance in 1960, the same year he became a partner. He had solid credentials—both a law degree and an MBA—and a polished but detached manner. More than a few people in the firm were put off by his aloofness, even though Jerry was not consciously arrogant. Basically, he was cerebral by nature, which didn't easily mesh with Cy's trader's temperament and locker-room banter. Also, he had developed an investment banking methodology that was evidently too novel to be properly appreciated by Cy.

In the late sixties, Jerry and a pair of protégés, Henry Kravis and George Roberts, began pursuing what they called bootstrap investments—what later became famously known as leveraged buyouts. They identified family-owned industrial companies whose founders were ready to retire and were willing to be bought out (so long as their competitors weren't the buyers). These were highly leveraged deals with the acquired company's assets providing the collateral for the buyout loans. Bear Stearns would provide some of the financing, but most of it came from private investors, banks, and institutions. New management would be installed, payrolls trimmed, efficiency increased, stand-alone divisions sold off, and Kohlberg (or Kravis or Roberts) would assume an active role on the board of directors. In the ideal scenario, at some point the surviving streamlined core business would be sold at multiples of the initial equity investment.

The payoffs from such deals far exceeded those for garden-variety underwritings, but the lead time for putting one together was much longer. Jerry knew that he was positioned to add enormous value to the investment banking franchise, but he also recognized that increasingly he and Kravis and Roberts were isolating themselves from the other partners. Their hands-on roles in the acquired companies regularly took them away from the office. Cy couldn't resist making cutting remarks about how they were out dillydallying when they should have been at their desks. (What Cy imagined they could have been doing more profitably sitting next to a phone I have no idea.) Probably the biggest obstacle was that most of the people in corporate finance preferred working with Sig. In the end, Jerry recognized that it made more sense to go off on his own, and Kravis and Roberts naturally went with him. Could the subsequent success of the firm Kohlberg, Kravis & Roberts—one of the most dazzling Wall Street stories of the latter twentieth century—have been possible under the auspices of Bear Stearns? I honestly don't know. Could their defection have been avoided or at least delayed? Though I have very little interest in hypothetical questions, I do fault both myself and Johnny for not doing more to keep Jerry, Henry Kravis, and George Roberts within the firm. Johnny and I discussed this on many occasions. We were wrong. It might not have worked, but we should have tried harder. As much as Johnny and others labored to fill the vacuum left by their departure, we never fully managed to do so.

Ironically, by the time Jerry resigned, in March 1976, Cy's day-to-day role and stature had faded to a shadow. Physically he'd become a mess—overweight, over-drinking—and he seemed to spend a lot of time living in the past. In 1978 he announced his retirement as senior partner. Every April we held our annual partners' dinner at the Harmonie Club, and we decided to turn that year's gathering into a valedictory ceremony of sorts. Cy intended to continue coming to the office, in an emeritus capacity. Slipping away unobtrusively would have been out of character for him, and you could say that he didn't disappoint. When the moment in the evening arrived for ritual testimonials, Cy was presented with a wrapped package. Inside was an expensive wristwatch, but he never laid eyes on it. As he attempted to unwrap it he struggled for a few moments, then fell over backwards. He'd suffered a massive stroke. When the ambulance attendants had taken him away, I told everyone that Cy unquestionably would have wanted us to stay, have a couple of drinks in his honor, reminisce about him, and go home — certainly not abruptly break up the party. He died two days later, never having regained consciousness.

There is no question that Cy transformed Bear Stearns from a small commission house to a risk-taking machine. He did it by himself, against the wishes of some of his superiors. For that, he deserves all the credit in the world.

6

Six months after cy lewis's death, Ted Low passed away—concessions to the most basic law of nature that led me to consider an odd existential (or maybe metaphysical, or meta-fiscal?) notion. I'd noticed that partners in investment firms inevitably grew old and died, but I hadn't given thought to how, in the process, they actually defied another law of nature. Lo and behold, they actually *could* take it with them. Sort of. Between them, Cy and Ted had held roughly 50 percent of Bear Stearns's capital, and their estates were entitled to receive all of this money over five years. We also had three years to go to complete the payout of Jerry Kohlberg's interest. In deference to the strains that Cy's demise had placed upon our liquidity, Jerry had graciously proposed stopping the clock until we had replenished our capital—a class act by a class guy that I'll never forget. We never took him up on this. Still, we were in a dicey situation and knew it; a couple of untimely pedestrian-bus mishaps could have put us on the ropes.

I'd already had a glimpse of my own mortality and it had left an indelible impression. When I was thirty-one, I had a wife, a child, another on the way, an overfull plate, and—I learned one day in a doctor's office—colon cancer. Until I'd started bleeding, I'd had no clue that anything was wrong.

The survival rate for colon cancer in those days was alarmingly low. When I told my parents they said, "You're going to the Mayo Clinic," and they went with me. The first doctor there who examined me asked how I felt. Terrific, I said. He asked how I'd spent my weekend. Playing golf and bridge, I told him. "Well, that's interesting," he said, "because you don't seem to have any blood in your veins. You're going to have some tests now. And we're operating tomorrow."

The surgery went fine, but the recovery did not. I became very sick with a staph infection, something I'd never even heard of. For about ten days I was desperately ill—enough that I told my parents good-bye. And then I started getting better. Right there, in the hospital, I vowed that for the rest of my life I would do whatever I wanted, as long as I didn't hurt anyone else physically, mentally, or spiritually. At the top of the list was returning home to my family and to Bear Stearns. Ever since, unless I've been on vacation I've never missed a day of work, and that includes the time I returned from a safari in Africa with malaria.

Over the next few years, I found the time to immerse myself in many of my youthful enthusiasms. When I was eight years old, I had witnessed the celebrated stage illusionist Harry Blackstone Sr. at a theater on Main Street, in downtown Oklahoma City. A few months later, on a family trip to Dallas during the Texas Centennial celebration, my parents wisely realized that exposing me to the exotic art of Sally Rand could have lasting educational value. I decided that magic and fan dancing would be my two hobbies—doing one and watching the other. As a teenager I often did magic at parties, an indication that I was the sort of dauntless amateur who eagerly performs for just about any audience, so long as they're breathing.

Gail Borden
Public Library District
www.gailborden.info

Customer ID: **********3596

Items that you checked out

Title:
 The rise and fall of Bear Stearns / Alan
 C. Greenberg with Mark Singer.
ID: 31113011883414
Due: Tuesday, September 06, 2016

Total items: 1
Account balance: $0.00
8/8/2016 3:06 PM
Checked out: 1
Overdue: 0
Hold requests: 0
Ready for pickup: 0

Please remember to return materials on
time; others are waiting to enjoy them as
well.

Renew by phone - 847-742-3210
Renew online - gailborden.info/account

In New York, I took lessons from Slydini, one of the all-time great sleight-of-hand masters, and I hung out on Saturday afternoons with the group of magicians that for decades occupied the back room of Reuben's Restaurant, on Madison Avenue. Each year I'd give a performance to benefit the Boy Scouts of America. Any nonprofit organization—the Boys Club, the Jewish Home and Hospital, whomever—that asked me to do the same for them didn't have to twist my arm. For the annual Bear Stearns children's holiday party I tried to pull out all the stops. Any encouragement I got from that crowd meant a lot to me. I did an effect with peanut butter and jelly that usually went over well. That took some of the sting out of knowing that I would momentarily be upstaged by Brutus, my hurdle-jumping ten-inch-high Papillon. I'd like to believe that every kid who showed up for the holiday party did so voluntarily.

The first magic book I ever acquired, *Blackstone's Card Tricks and Modern Magic,* I borrowed from a friend who lived on my block in Oklahoma City—an inadvertent long-term loan. It's one of thousands of books and tapes about magic that share shelf space in my apartment along with my extensive collections of other books reflecting my avocational interests: natural history, fishing, archery, dog training, golf. (Contrary to what you might expect of someone in my line of work, I own no books on the art of war or hand-to-hand combat. I did have a brief dalliance with martial arts that began when Johnny Rosenwald and I signed up for judo lessons at the Harmonie Club. I stayed with that, as I recall, until I'd received my yellow belt, which they gave you for being able to tie the belt properly around your judo robe.)

My father used to take me fishing when I was small. I loved it, and when I attended summer camp in Missouri I learned how to use a fly rod, which I've been doing, mostly in Colorado or Wyoming or upstate New York, ever since. Presenting a dry fly from twenty-five yards away with the precision necessary to bamboozle a wary trout is one of the sublime rewards of angling. But for about as long as I've been hooking them I've routinely felt overmatched by the logistics of netting fish that refuse to cooperate—which eventually inspired the development of the Greenberg Grab, my revolutionary method for landing a feisty rainbow while wading in a swift current. A few years ago, Peter Kaminsky, the fly-fishing columnist for the *New York Times,* wrote an approving column about the Greenberg Grab. I won't go into all the fine points, other than to say that it requires an understanding of fulcrums and levers. Peter stopped short of nominating me for a Nobel Prize in physics, but he clearly admired my resourcefulness.

I was able to hone my archery skills at summer camp, but I had previously gotten started at home. When I was about ten I asked my father for a BB rifle and he absolutely refused. I had a fallback plan: "Okay, how about a bow and arrow?" As always, he had a logical response: "Well, I guess I've never heard of anyone being shot with an unloaded bow and arrow." I did target practice in our backyard and taught archery when I worked as a counselor at the camp, then lapsed for several years, and took it up again seriously after my cancer surgery. I have no interest in hunting with a rifle, but I bow-hunted on three African safaris in the sixties and seventies. Trophies from those trips—a waterbuck, a greater kudu, and a nyala— hang on the walls of the same room that contains the bulk of my magic books. There's also a cobra-shaped horn that belonged to a water buffalo. Because it wasn't a clean kill, I felt it wouldn't have been right to mount the entire head.

For many years, I have been a trustee of the American Museum of Natural History. I've collected a lot of books on zoology because I've always been fascinated by natural evolution and adaptability. I've been asked whether there isn't a logical contradiction between hunting and my genuine love of animals, especially dogs. The answer is that: (a) I really love dogs, I have since I was a small boy, I've rarely met a well-bred dog that failed to engage me at least as much as the average human, and (b) what I love about animals in general, especially quadrupeds, is that they don't spend a lot of time second-guessing themselves. Survival doesn't allow for that. Observing a kudu or a water buffalo or, for that matter, a woodchuck in the wild is to recognize that they live through action—a trait emulated by anyone who trades successfully on a daily basis, whether he realizes it or not.

Canines are more cerebral than armadillos, but you rarely encounter one that thwarts you by overthinking the situation at hand. I got serious about dog training in my late thirties, starting with a Doberman. I had a lot of success with Willie, a toy poodle that was certified by the American Kennel Club (AKC) as a "tracking dog"—the only toy poodle trained in Central Park to earn that distinction. The results were more mixed with Herzl, a Canaan, an Israeli breed that, five years after I began entering him in dog shows, was officially recognized by the AKC. I thought that was broad-minded of the AKC, in light of the fact that Herzl's competitive career was short-circuited by his tendency to bite strangers. When Herzl was thirteen he bit someone in Central Park and I finally decided to have him euthanized. I took him to a veterinarian, said good-bye, went to my office, and told everyone that Herzl was dead, only to get a call from the vet a few hours later explaining that I needed to come pick up Herzl because, by New York law, any dog that bites someone has to be kept alive for ten days. I figured out that if Herzl bit someone every nine days he'd probably live to be about twenty.

Brutus, who died several years ago, was one of a pair of Papillons I owned at the time. He was a marvelous performer who, in one show, received the title of both utility dog and champion. "Utility" is the AKC's highest level of obedience, and "champion" designates the highest level of beauty. That was a very happy day in my family's life, although Brutus seemed quite nonchalant. Despite his résumé, I once had to go to great lengths to rehabilitate his reputation with the AKC after he bit a judge who had handled his testicles in a way that Brutus found objectionable. To his credit, Brutus almost immediately seemed willing to let bygones be bygones. There's probably a business parable in that.

In any event, I've never read a case study of a dog becoming depressed over forgetting where he buried a bone. Nor am I prone to hand-wringing over last week's red ink, literal or figurative. The famous dictum about those who fail to remember the past being condemned to repeat it makes sense, but being hostage to the past is hardly a winning proposition. From my earliest days at Bear Stearns I'd appreciated that an arbitrageur or trader thrived by being wide awake, nimble, and decisive in real time. After Cy and Ted died, when the challenge to replenish our capital presented itself, the imperative was simple: the moment to get *seriously* busy was upon us. The major burden rested on my shoulders. I felt that I needed to come up with some motivational message that, by revealing previously undisclosed insights into how to make money, would galvanize our 1,200 employees. Miraculously (if not exactly by pure coincidence), it was then that I made the acquaintance of the dean of business philosophers, Haimchinkel Malintz Anaynikal, a humble sage of modern capitalism and management.

For the next twenty-three years I routinely dispatched inner-office memoranda that invoked Haimchinkel's pithiest and shrewdest maxims, reminders of ways in which we could generate more revenue, better serve our clients, enhance morale, and control our overhead (an idiosyncratic obsession of Haimchinkel's and mine). After about ten years, H.M.A.'s nephew and protégé, Itzhak Nanook Pumpernickanaylian, a.k.a. "Nookie," pitched in. Like all gurus, Haimchinkel frequently spoke in metaphors. Refreshingly, his tended to be bluntly colorful rather than cryptically obscure.

They also possessed a more poetic ring than most of my lapel-grabbing exhortations. In one of my early communiqués, in the fall of 1978, I explained that it's difficult to run a business if the partners aren't able to get in touch with each other. I had a simple standard: if you're going to be away from your desk for more than ten minutes, make sure that a fellow employee knows where you are. I cited a study of 200 Wall Street firms that were no longer in business, which had found that 62.349 percent had gone bust because their employees chronically violated the ten-minute rule—a statistic, by the way, that took me roughly ten seconds to invent. My point: "That idiocy will not occur here." Slow learners, I warned, ran the risk of being outfitted with "bulky and not very attractive" radio collars previously owned by the St. Louis Zoo.

Similarly, I decreed how long it should take to return a phone call from a colleague or customer: immediately was satisfactory, failing to do so by the end of the workday flat-out unacceptable. I *was* willing to make an exception if the dilatory call returner had an extreme emergency—say, dying during lunch. Otherwise I didn't hesitate to fulfill the role of tough cop. Capital punishment for repeat offenders? Bear Stearns had an in-house rule barring execution devices in the workplace, so that really wasn't an option.

Haimchinkel, as I've suggested, had a lighter touch. In March 1979, when we decided to raise fresh capital by offering limited partnerships to Gus Ring and others, I reported this in a memo to the incumbent general and limited partners. Things were looking up on several fronts, a state of affairs that always made me wary. I reminded the partners: "You know how I feel about the dangers of overconfidence." Haimchinkel's corollary advice was more quotable: "Thou will do well in commerce as long as thou does not believe thine own odor is perfume." I found this adage so evocative that I shamelessly recycled it—ad nauseam—across the years.

In time a book emerged from this extended endeavor, *Memos from the Chairman.* The notion of binding my interoffice correspondence between hard covers never would have occurred to me. It happened because one of our salesmen, David Workman, had shared several examples with his brother, Peter, who runs a very successful publishing house. Thanks to Workman Publishing, *Memos from the Chairman* has never gone out of print. According to Amazon.com, it has remained consistently in demand, credit for which I've been more than happy to share with Haimchinkel and Nookie. (But not the royalties; those have all gone to a college scholarship fund I created for the relatives of Bear Stearns employees. Actually, I set up two such funds. The first began with a $500,000 gift to New York University in 1984, an endowment reserved for undergraduates who had a relative working in our New York office. I subsequently added $700,000, and now, even with all the grants that have been made, the endowment totals more than $1.5 million. Feeling that I'd been remiss in not doing something comparable for the branch offices, I gave $300,000 to establish the second fund. The book royalties all went there. Haimchinkel and Nookie, philanthropic fellows themselves, were good sports about this.)

A lot of my memos began with a bulletin that the month or quarter or year just completed had been the "best" or most profitable in the firm's history. These were statements of fact, never hyperbole. Every time I shared such news I warned of the dangers of complacency, cockiness, sloppiness, carelessness, and relaxing on expenses. In a rising market, Haimchinkel would always chime in with a reminder that markets can and will make unexpected U-turns: "When the going gets tough, the tough start selling." Indeed.

Our continuous expansion—between 1973 and 1981, for example, we went from 700 to 2,600 employees, and seven years after that were up to 6,000—provided frequent opportunities to reiterate core principles, one of which was that we were and would remain a meritocracy with a built-in farm team. Graduate business schools from all over were minting shiny new MBAs. A huge proportion of them, instead of following the usual path to corporate managerial careers, were flocking to Wall Street brokerage and investment banking firms. "There has been a lot of publicity lately about firms hiring students with MBA degrees," I wrote in the spring of 1981. "Our first desire is to promote from within. If somebody with an MBA degree applies for a job, we will certainly not hold it against them, but we are really looking for people with PSD degrees." (Translation: "poor, smart and a deep desire to become rich.")

In an ideal scenario, the "D" in PSD would manifest itself as a sensibly focused competitiveness. We hired smart aggressive people with the expectation that smart aggressive people would hire more smart aggressive people. (Dummies, likewise, beget dummies.) When the smart people came up with ideas for well-conceived business opportunities, we said go for it. As always, organizational charts, management consultants, and business plans played virtually no role in any of this. My own strategic thinking I did mostly while showering or shaving.

Not surprisingly, as we added new talent and branched into new areas or broadened our activities in others— government bonds, mortgage-backed securities, a much wider range of municipal bonds—my management style was tested. Even with all of my sermonizing about controlling costs and the necessity for humility, I found that whenever things seemed to be going awfully well, laxity would waltz in. And when I saw or sensed that happening I didn't hesitate to brandish the unveiled threat, as in: "I would like to announce at this time a freeze on expenses and carelessness. We probably throw away millions every year on stupidities and slop. The next associate of mine that does something 'un-neat' is going to have a little meeting with me and I will not be the usual charming, sweet, understanding, pleasant, entertaining, affable yokel from Oklahoma."

I hatched various self-policing initiatives. Every morning I would look at what we called flash reports, printouts that listed trades above $200,000 that we had handled the previous day for our clearing customers. Another daily report showed trades by our employees for their personal accounts. If I noticed that someone was doing a lot of buying and selling, I called his boss and asked, "What's with this guy?" A person who's buying and selling that same day is gambling in the stock market, which means he's going to lose his shirt.

No one, especially myself, wanted an atmosphere in which colleagues viewed each other with suspicion. Rather, the goal was a collective commitment to running the tightest possible ship. If the guy at the next desk was spending every weekend in Atlantic City, that had a bearing upon his behavior and performance the other five days of the week—and by extension had a potential effect upon our bottom line.

Peccadilloes large and small would elude me, naturally, which was why I depended upon others at Bear Stearns to observe what was happening in their immediate vicinities. A couple of mornings a week I conspicuously took a brisk tour of our headquarters, my way of signaling to the troops that their leader was one of them—and also that he was minding the store by keeping an eye on them. I always had the same destination, the area where our retail representatives worked. Along the way I said hi to everyone I passed, and it was understood that any employee who wanted to tell me or ask me something was welcome to do so. Most of those exchanges lasted about as long as my patented now-you-hear-me-now-you-don't phone conversations, but when I could, I referred the employee to someone who would be able to answer a question in detail.

Every Monday I chaired a meeting of the risk committee, whose agenda was to enforce limits on the extent of our capital exposure. Traders from eight or ten departments attended knowing that yours truly would react quite unhappily if anyone was found to be holding a loss. As a rule, losing positions got sold on Friday, and I didn't care how nasty a hit we had to take, by 4:00 p.m. Monday all the dogs better have been off the books.

The reasons traders would give for their reluctance to bite the bullet could never rid the room of the stink of burning

71

money. They would explain that some institution had to raise cash quickly and had driven down the price of a stock or bond. Or: "The chairman's making a presentation to analysts next Thursday. Let's hold on until then."

"What do you think he's gonna say?" I'd tell them. "He'll give some line of baloney. You know, I'm single these days"— my first marriage had ended in the mid-seventies; in 1987, I married Kathryn Olson, which was the smartest thing I've ever done—"Do you think I'd take out any girl based only on her father's recommendation? You've got a loss. Take it. If you want to buy it back in a week, okay."

In every single case they would not buy it back. The trader would walk around like a load had been lifted off his head. He was so glad he didn't have to look at that open sore on his position book.

It could well have been something in my DNA that, as Cy Lewis had so felicitously put it, enabled me to treat securities like toilet paper. Still, I never stopped being amazed that some traders, whose own DNA might have been to blame, would apparently fall in love with certain stocks or bonds. To guard against that, we set trading limits that stipulated the amount of capital a trader could commit to a position. Not that that could prevent even my most disciplined protégés from occasionally convincing themselves that an exception should be made. Once, during the early 1980s, when there was a surge of merger activity in the energy industry, Bobby Steinberg, who had taken over risk arbitrage, tried to make the case for buying a bigger block of a takeover target than the limits allowed. His reason? "I *really* like this one," he told Alan Schwartz, who was then the head of the investment banking department. Alan volunteered to intervene with me. The conversation was brief. I told him, "Let me ask you something, Alan:

do you think we have these limits to keep people from buying things they *don't* really like?"

The unpardonable taboo for a trader was to bury a loss while waiting wishfully for the price to recover. Our compliance officers—Sy the Spy, the Ferret, and the Snoop (not the names their parents gave them but real people nonetheless)—had the task of ensuring that none of our positions was marked incorrectly. Every day they circulated though the various departments, spread out over several floors, randomly approaching traders. When they said, "Let me see your book," the trader had no choice but to comply. The Spy, the Ferret, or the Snoop would then spend a day or so checking every position and price. If any trader put up the slightest resistance, I was to be notified at once. "It'll make my day," I promised.

Whistle-blowing was never frowned upon. "We want the people at Bear Stearns to cry wolf," I once wrote. "If the doubt is justified, the reporter will be handsomely rewarded. If the suspicion proves unfounded, the person who brought it to our attention will be thanked for his or her vigilance and told to keep it up." Somewhat later I declared that anyone who disclosed a potential negative mismark would collect 5 percent of the buried loss. For those who felt uneasy about taking the reward money, we'd give it to their favorite charity. Essentially I was imploring all of us, as I put it more than once, "not to bankrupt this golden goose." That same impetus inspired my most dazzling (if I do say so) innovation, the stroke of brilliance (if I may again) that became as closely identified with my management practices as any decision I ever made. In the summer of 1985, less than three months before our initial public offering, I wrote, "Bear Stearns is probably going to sell stock to the public, and there is one guarantee that

I would like to give potential buyers of our stock—they are going to get the fairest shake from us that management can give any public shareholder. This place is going to be run tight and the reasons are not altruistic . . . we want the stock to appreciate." Accordingly, I had "just informed the purchasing department that they should no longer purchase paper clips." Instead we would endlessly recycle the little critters already dwelling among us. Also, we would radically cut back on the purchase of blue envelopes used for interoffice mail, given that strategic licking (and a casualness about hygiene) could make it possible to reuse those envelopes many times. Soon my paper-clip and envelope-hoarding fixations extended to rubber bands. (Broken rubber bands could be rejuvenated by tying the ends together. For the uninitiated, I suggested a session with an arbitrageur who was available to demystify the art of the square knot.) In subsequent years, I would also be nudged towards apoplexy by the heedless proliferation of fax machines. Light switches left on after hours, same thing. Later yet, I devised a scheme to enable the firm to retain the rights to frequent-flyer miles accumulated by employees during business travel. Was it my ambition to gain notoriety as an administrative tightwad? Absolutely.

The paper-clip-envelope-rubber-band sideshow was less frivolous than it appeared. A public offering by a then-sixty-two-year-old Wall Street partnership would undoubtedly arouse plenty of press attention. I wanted it to extol our not-widely-enough-appreciated reputation for being neither profligate nor elitist, and I think that message did proliferate. In the years that followed, I occasionally fantasized about the beneficial effect my paper-clip fanaticism had upon our stock price. I know for certain that it didn't hurt.

●　●　●

On october 16, 1987, a Friday, I circulated a lighthearted memo that consisted mostly of trusty chestnuts from Haimchinkel. No oracular revelations, though I did enjoy his definition of merchant banking, a term whose meaning had always eluded me. "Merchant banking," he explained, "is buying stock in a company whose shares are not publicly traded and the company should be in a business very different from what you are familiar with." An excellent place to stash your money, in other words, if you didn't mind never seeing it again. Three days later came Black Monday. The Dow went over a cliff—508 points, or 22.6 percent—the most dramatic one-day decline in history. Once the market closed, I knew it was incumbent upon me to offer some reassurance and perspective.

"It is amazing how history keeps repeating itself," I wrote. "The market in stocks and bonds has taken a precipitous drop, but I am far from depressed. Why? Because once again we are seeing and we will be seeing great opportunities in all areas, particularly in personnel. I can assure you we are pursuing every lead at this very moment." This had always been a preferred recruiting ploy; when the market plummeted, we could cherry-pick PSDs who, usually through no fault of their own, were looking for work. I pointed out that markets such as this also brought out the worst in some people. To illustrate, I appended a fictitious press release that an anonymous misanthrope had sent to the media, reporting Haimchinkel's death, attributable to "acute overexposure." Its depiction of me, allegedly the sole honorary pallbearer and mourner at his funeral, howling in despair, plainly didn't ring true. I in fact remained my equable self, even when the Dow dropped another 10 percent the following day.

Once, when the bond markets were in a prolonged slump,

I took a phone call from a reporter who wanted to know how Bear Stearns had been affected. I told him, "You can't fly with the eagles and poop like a canary." This time around, the *New York Times* asked me to contribute to an article featuring analyses from an assortment of financial and economic eminences. I rewarded them with one of my deeply considered insights: "Markets fluctuate. Next question."

The main danger we faced was a consequence of so many of the brokerage firms we cleared for having gone broke literally overnight. Their customers had made trades that hadn't yet settled and nobody could say what the stocks and bonds were worth. Five days later, when all deliveries had to be completed, what would we be stuck with? Stocks that we'd held for our own account we just sold and took the hit. And we unavoidably took another hit once the clearing trades settled, but much less wounding than I'd feared. Our customers had also held options, both long and short, that it would have been prohibitively expensive to cover. The main exposure was with puts that clients had sold. By sitting on those until the contracts expired, by which time reality had reasserted itself, the losses we sustained were much more modest than we'd initially anticipated.

What few people now realize about Black Monday is that the market bottomed out the same week it crashed. It took a couple of years to complete the recovery, and some stocks never did. In November 1987, we moved from downtown to midtown, 55 Water Street to 245 Park Avenue, where we had space to grow. We needed it. Our fixed costs would be higher and, as I predicted, by spring we had hired three hundred new people. All the more reason, as Haimchinkel and I refused to stop harping, to keep a lid on other costs.

Black Monday did produce one unexpected windfall for

Bear Stearns. A few weeks before the crash, we had signed an agreement to sell a big chunk of the company to the Jardine Matheson Group, a Hong Kong–based outfit owned by a British family named Keswick. Since going public, our stock had split four times. In the initial offering, 33 percent of it had been reserved for our partners. Jardine wanted to acquire about that large a stake, but because we had recently chartered a commercial bank in New Jersey, the regulators wouldn't let us sell more than 25 percent. So we made a deal with Jardine that called for them to make a tender offer for 25 percent of Bear Stearns's shares in the open market. Whatever the public didn't tender, we promised our original partners would sell from our personal holdings. Black Monday had triggered a plunge in stock markets around the world. The exchange in Hong Kong was so blindsided it shut down for four days, during which Jardine's shares fell sufficiently that it made more sense for them to buy back their own shares than to buy ours. The Keswick brothers, Simon and Henry, who controlled Jardine, wanted to call the whole thing off. We didn't and filed a lawsuit, but not before Arthur Liman, the lawyer who represented us in the original sale agreement (and who was considered one of the most skillful litigators in the country), tried to talk me out of it. We would probably lose the case on summary judgment, he advised.

I said, "Arthur, so what? Is there some kind of terrible thing about losing a summary judgment? Does that mean I'm not going to be able to get into some country club?"

The next summer I took a vacation in Aspen, Colorado. While waiting to tee off one morning, I found myself seated on a bench next to one of Jardine's chief financial officers. We had an entirely friendly conversation that concluded with him saying, "All right, let's settle this thing—$3 million," and me saying, "We'll see you in court." I was referring specifically to the uninviting New York State Supreme Court, in lower Manhattan, where rumor had it the bathrooms had last been mopped during the Dewey administration. We all found the Keswick brothers to be likable gents, especially if you liked to hunt grouse and wear tweed knickers. Two days into the trial they announced that they wanted to settle. When the judge came up with a number we could live with—$60 million—the Keswicks recoiled. What finally brought them around was our promise never to drag them to that courthouse again. A couple of years later one of the Keswicks inquired whether we could possibly perhaps terribly-sorry-to-trouble-you consider hiring his son for the summer. We could.

For all the tears shed and money that vaporized in the aftermath of Black Monday, for all of my worldly understanding of how markets can betray even the most scrupulous investors, that crash provided no frame of reference for the devastation that awaited two decades down the road. By 1991, four major firms—E. F. Hutton, Thomson MacKinnon, L. F. Rothschild, and Drexel Burnham—had gone out of business. Three others, Bache, First Boston and Kidder Peabody, would not have survived if they hadn't been bailed out by their parent companies (respectively Prudential, Credit Suisse, and General Electric). When I published *Memos from the Chairman* in 1996, I pointed out that the price tag of those rescues had come to $3.5 billion, an amount that I found appalling and astonishing.

And which now, far more astonishingly, seems to me utterly quaint.

CHAPTER 7

For the same reasons that i went to such lengths to be accessible on the trading floor and else-where in our main office, I made it a point to meet prospec-tive new employees, especially during the years when we were building up the retail side of the business. I would spend fif-teen minutes listening, answering questions, explaining why Bear Stearns was such a challenging and rewarding place to pursue a career. We're growing, we need fresh blood and energy, come aboard—that was gist of my proselytizing and it usually worked. Some of the people who joined the firm didn't stick around for long, which was bound to happen, but most of our decisions across the years proved out.

"Look, I work for you," I would tell new hires.

And they would always laugh and say, "Are you kidding?"

"No, I mean it. I'm part of the furniture here. You can quit. I can't."

That would get another laugh. Then I'd tell them my phone number and say, "If I can help you, I want to. I'm someone who's known for getting things done around here. When my phone rings I answer it myself. If you have a problem and you don't call me, it's not my fault."

A long-ago Bear Stearns summer intern told a friend of mine that he had met me his first day on the job, I'd shaken his hand, and said "Try to keep us liquid, kid," and that was the entire conversation. I'm sure that's an accurate recollection. Staying liquid was something I always did encourage.

One winter day in 1969 I got a call from Harold C. Mayer Jr., saying that he wanted to introduce me to someone he thought we should hire as a retail broker. I went to his office and had my first encounter with James E. Cayne—a self-assured fellow in his mid-thirties who worked for Lebenthal & Company, a municipal bond firm. We exchanged the usual pleasantries and he mentioned that he was a competitive bridge player, which interested me because I'd been playing since college and my game had long since hit a middling plateau. "How good are you?" I asked.

"I'll put it this way," he said. "If you play for the rest of your life, if you really work at it and play with great partners, you'll never be as good as I am now."

That, in my estimation, was a good sign. We were looking for PSDs—even though I hadn't yet coined that phrase—and Jimmy's brash confidence suggested that he was a live one. He grew up in Chicago, the son of a patent attorney, attended Purdue University but didn't graduate, got drafted and sent to Japan, came back to Chicago and drove a taxi, eloped with the sister of a Purdue fraternity brother, sold photocopiers in Utah and the Pacific Northwest, worked in his wife's family's scrap metal business, and left that after getting divorced. In 1964 he moved to New York and became, more or less, a bridge bum. Not many people could make a living as bridge professionals in those days, and Jimmy wasn't among them, but he played in lots of tournaments and occasionally won. Before going to work for Lebenthal, he had a job selling adding machines. None of his previous employment necessarily qualified him to become a retail municipal bond broker, but it didn't hurt that he was a natural salesman. He had a sense of humor and could connect easily with his customers, many of whom he'd met at the bridge table. Coming to work for us would allow him to sell stocks as well as bonds. No one sized Jimmy up as a trader—I didn't, anyway, and I don't recall him expressing that ambition—but he was adept at selling whatever we had in inventory. In building upon our early reputation as a streetwise bond-trading house, we had adhered to fundamentals: knowing our customers, finding the bonds (can't move the goods unless you have the goods), indulging no illusions about potential upsides and downsides. We joined underwriting syndicates to float corporate, municipal, and government issues, always mindful of the possible risks of getting stuck with paper that we had no desire to hold in our own account. Our general corporate-bond strategy was to steer clear of AAA-rated securities. We wouldn't hesitate to buy if we knew that we could quickly flip a block of bonds to an institutional customer, but the highest-rated bonds were the least likely to be marked down, so profit margins on them rarely made such trading worthwhile. During the sixties and seventies we did quite well by ignoring the herd and betting on lower-rated corporates—not junk bonds (a term that hadn't yet entered the lexicon) but oversold stuff. Often these were issued by conglomerates (Ling-Temco-Vought, Loews, Gulf+Western) and sold at deep discounts. Our track record persuaded us that they were far less risky than the market insisted, and we almost never got burned.

But our precautions and rigor and smarts couldn't spare us entirely from having to relearn lessons you would have thought we had already absorbed. One much-too-close-for-comfort episode occurred in 1975, when a New York state agency called the Urban Development Corporation (UDC) defaulted. The UDC had been created in 1968 and enjoyed a unique authority to finance major urban renewal ventures. It eventually had big hits with mega-developments such as Roosevelt Island and Battery Park City, but in 1975 a number of its low-income housing projects that were supposed to be self-sustaining had become fiscally unviable. The economy was mired in the worst recession since the Second World War — stagnant growth, inflation driven by OPEC oil prices, and interest rates nudging towards double digits. The finances of the City of New York and the State of New York amounted to an unfunny joke, the lame punch line of a long tradition of political farce and preposterous accounting.

On October 30, 1975, the New York *Daily News* published its instant-classic headline "Ford to City: Drop Dead," the verdict on Gerald Ford's unwillingness to help New York City stave off bankruptcy. The first harbinger of bankruptcy had occurred eight months earlier and Bear Stearns had had an unwanted front-row seat. On February 26, the state and the major banks settled upon a financing plan to prevent the UDC from collapsing. It was a complex agreement made possible by astute statecraft on the part of Governor Hugh Carey. Amazingly, though, no grown-ups had been minding the store the day before, when the state legislature refused to appropriate the money to pay off more than $100 million in UDC notes that had come due. At that moment default occurred and we — this was precisely the sort of surprise I despised — were among the UDC's most exposed bondholders.

For more than a decade our municipal bond department had been run by two smart and skilled traders, Howard Finney and Gene Marx. Both had retired, unfortunately, and their successor was either unaware or didn't bother telling the rest of us that two species of UDC bonds existed, one guaranteed by the state and the other backed by the state's "moral obligation." Guess which type we owned. Not that we had planned to. We found ourselves in that position because the previous year we had joined an underwriting syndicate led by a major New York City bank. The underwriting hadn't gone well and the syndicate members were saddled with more than $50 million worth (at par, anyway) of unsold bonds that were due to mature in twelve months. Once the market got wind of UDC's difficulties, the price behaved accordingly.

Normally we would have taken our bonds and swallowed our loss—assuming that God would have sent us some bottom-feeding speculators—but instead we found ourselves in a peculiar predicament. The lead bank in the syndicate, which had no desire to acknowledge its own loss, had offered to lend us the face value of our bonds at an interest rate slightly below the coupon rate. That way we could earn a small premium while waiting out the year. Inevitably, though, the gloomy outlook for the UDC, the state, and the city made it impossible to ignore that the state's moral obligation was basically worthless. Next: (a) the lead bank announced that it was breaking up our syndicate and handed over our share of the bonds, (b) the UDC defaulted, and (c) we discovered that the lead bank had expropriated UDC funds that it already had on deposit, the equivalent of a collateral seizure.

The bank transacted this last stunt without any forewarning to the rest of the syndicate. The ensuing lawsuit we filed was not something we did for sport. We had been pegging our capital at less than $25 million, but that figure was based upon book values of some problematic assets. If we'd been brutally honest about actual values, a $10 million loss on the bonds would have been devastating. A month later, Governor Carey cajoled the legislature to back the UDC bonds and the immediate crisis passed. We got paid in full and dropped our lawsuit. One consequence of the UDC near-death experience was that from that point on, every partner would receive every Monday morning a copy of every one of our bond and equity positions; theoretically, none of us would ever again be ignorant of our risk exposure.

Throughout 1975, the saga of New York City's precarious finances resembled an old radio or silent-film serial melodrama: cliffhangers, brinksmanship, low behavior, scheming, isolated heroics. The heads of Chase Manhattan, Citibank, and Morgan Guaranty paid a courtesy call to Governor Carey to give notice that they would no longer lend money to the city, period. Formal bankruptcy was averted only when the city was placed in receivership, with the state in the role of trustee. Since moral-obligation reassurances had become obsolete, the rescuing entity, the Municipal Assistance Corporation (MAC), issued bonds that attracted buyers only because they were guaranteed by earmarked New York state revenues. For a fee, New York City notes could be exchanged for MAC bonds. As always, the key was to find the notes. Because we'd been making a market in them—stuff that most Wall Street firms wouldn't touch—this became a lucrative sideline for us. In various ways, the historical details of this episode are instructive.

Let me fast-forward then back up: A while back I read a statement by Jimmy Cayne that I had enticed him to Bear Stearns with a $70,000 annual salary and that within a couple of years he was taking home $900,000 in commissions. I found this amusing for a moment, but that passed. The fact is that when we hired Jimmy as a registered rep he had to wait several months and take licensing exams before he was allowed to sell equities. In 1969, that meant starting at $700 per month. The $900,000 figment? I'll say this as politely as possible: *I think not.* Still, he did become a steady producer and in 1973 we made him a partner. His authority didn't extend beyond the retail department, but he hardly saw that as an obstacle to anything. Like any PSD, he wanted to get rich as expeditiously as possible, and from the start he systematically ingratiated himself with anyone he sized up as potentially useful in furthering his ambitions. As you would expect, from early on I was on his short list. Meanwhile, anyone who didn't make the cut knew it.

Before the MAC rescue materialized, an enormous oversupply of New York City debt obligations existed that, as I've mentioned, our usual competitors treated like kryptonite. At one point, Jimmy became aware that some of our retail customers owned short-term city notes two months shy of maturity that were being quoted at 97 cents on the dollar. It gave him a timely idea. He went to see the New York City employee responsible for investing municipal funds in overnight deposits at commercial banks and learned that the city was earning an annualized rate of return in the 2- to 3-percent range. If the city were to use that same money to invest in its own bonds, Jimmy explained, it could do much better. A bond due in sixty days that could be bought at 99 cents would yield 6 percent; if you paid 97 cents, the return would be 18 percent, and so on. Jimmy's suggestion was well-received. He next discussed it with me, Cy Lewis, and other partners, and we gave him the go-ahead. We would take out advertisements announcing that we were buying New York City paper. Yes, the banks might have frozen the city out of the credit market, but we were thawing the secondary market.

When Jimmy said to me, "We're advertising that we're buying these things, but who are we going to sell them to?" I told him not to worry, we'd find buyers. And we did. It was a very successful piece of business. Without question Jimmy had pushed this idea and deserved credit for bringing it to Cy's and my attention. But given that I'd been trading distressed and defaulted bonds for twenty-five years and Cy had been for forty—Jimmy and the registered reps worked on a different floor and did not trade anything—we would have figured it out on our own. The trading was done by me, along with our municipal bond department. I went to my biggest clients and found plenty of takers. (One, Gene Klein, who owned the San Diego Chargers, the National Football League franchise, called and asked me, "What do you like?" I told him we had New York City notes that were selling at sixty and headed to a hundred, he put in an order, and the next day he phoned back and reneged—the only time in sixty-one years that ever happened to me. That was also the last time I ever spoke to Gene Klein.)

None of these facts deterred Jimmy, many years later, from recounting this entire chain of events as a more or less singlehanded triumph by him, from conception to execution, that saved New York City from extinction. The truth—that he himself didn't buy or sell any of these notes—was evidently a trivial inconvenience.

I suppose because Jimmy's capacity for self-aggrandizement was still largely under wraps, what I failed to recognize at the time—I plead guilty to being slow on the uptake—were the lengths he would go to rewrite history, to spin a mythology that exaggerated his own accomplishments while diminishing the contributions of others. (But let's just say that I had long since wised up by the summer of 2007, when, to cite a case in point, as the events that would lead to our ruin were gathering momentum, Charles Gasparino, a correspondent for CNBC, published a sycophantic article in *Trader Monthly*,

All photographs courtesy of the author except for the photo of Salim (Cy) Lewis, which is by Bachrach Photography.

With my mother, Esther.

My family. Left to right: me; my brother, Maynard; my mother; my sister, DiAnne; my dad, Ted.

With my dad at a regional track meet in Oklahoma City, where I won the 100-yard and 220-yard dashes for the second consecutive year, 1945.

As a halfback at the University of Oklahoma, fall 1945.

Harold C. Mayer, one of the founders of Bear Stearns
and a great friend.

Early days on Wall Street. I am second from left.

With John Slade, my mentor at Bear Stearns.

With Mickey Tarnopol, a dear friend who brought a lot of business to Bear Stearns.

On the right is John Rosenwald, a close friend and the best salesman I have ever met. My sister, DiAnne Hirsch, is between us.

Salim (Cy) Lewis, my predecessor as head of Bear Stearns.

The Corporate America bridge team in London to play against the
bridge teams from the House of Lords and the House of Commons.
Left to right: Warren Buffett, Jimmy Cayne, Malcolm Forbes,
George Gillespie, me, Larry Tisch. A pretty well-to-do bunch.

MEMOS
FROM THE
CHAIRMAN

BY ALAN C. GREENBERG
WITH A FOREWORD BY
WARREN BUFFETT

The chairman of Bear Stearns is known throughout
the financial world for his biting, quirky, invariably
wise memos. And now, for the record, here is Ace
Greenberg on ethics, on telephone manners, on cycles
and trends, on being a contrarian, and on why he
spends so much time worrying about paper clips.

Memos from the Chairman.

With my wife, Kathy.
Our 1987 marriage was
the smartest thing I've
ever done in my life.
Kathy is an attorney
and chairman of the
board of Cardozo
School of Law.

With Kathy, my son, Teddy, and my daughter, Lynne.

With Teddy Kollek, at the time the mayor of Jerusalem, a great friend.

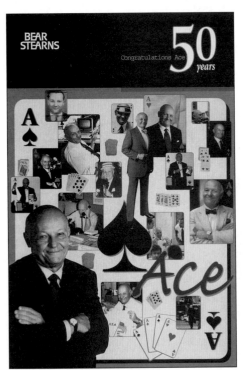

A poster that my colleagues at Bear Stearns made to celebrate my fifty years with the company.

a lifestyle magazine aimed at young Wall Street hotshots— the magazine and its catchy slogan, "See It, Make It, Spend It," are no longer with us—which described Jimmy as having "built Bear Stearns from the ground up, brick by brick." Could there have been anyone at Bear Stearns other than Jimmy himself who believed that? I didn't even bother sending a corrective letter to the editor.)

As it was, the Jimmy Cayne I dealt with in those early years struck me as high-energy, clever, and calculating (which I do not mean in a pejorative sense). He could make it rain, he had sharp political instincts, he proved to be a very effective proselytizer for Bear Stearns, and I generally found him entertaining to be around. Not long after he became a partner I altered my morning carpool arrangements. Instead of being imprisoned in Cy's car while listening to him and Ted Low pontificate and bloviate in the backseat, I began riding downtown with Jimmy. I'd been hoping for a reprise of my halcyon commuting days with Johnny Rosenwald and John Gutfreund, when a code of mutually respectful silence prevailed. That wasn't Jimmy's style, but eventually he had no choice but to accept that our conversations, as such, would be mostly one-sided. The more barbed the comments he volunteered about many of our fellow partners, the less I had to say. What did Jimmy make of my refusal to engage at that level? I didn't really care. In retrospect, I assume this ongoing ritual was part of some manipulation he was orchestrating in his Machiavellian fantasy life.

My divorce occurred in 1975 and, with extra time on my hands, I decided to focus more on my bridge game, enlisting Jimmy as my mentor. I applied the same standard I had when I wanted to hone my sleight-of-hand technique and sought out Slydini, the supreme virtuoso of "misdirection"—

diverting an audience's attention the instant before a sleight occurred. Not that Jimmy enjoyed a status in the bridge world in any way comparable to Slydini's in the magic world, but he seemed eminently qualified for my purposes. He had an impressive track record as a tournament competitor and years before he came to work at Bear Stearns he had become a life master in the American Contract Bridge League. At one point he told me that he'd decided to stop playing in tournaments because of the prevalence of cheating. My response was "Don't quit. Teach me and I'll become your partner." Jimmy tried to put me off—"Having you as my bridge partner might not enhance my future prospects at this firm," he said—but we quickly got past that.

Within a couple of years, our five-man team had won a national championship, the Reisinger Trophy, which qualified us for a four-team playoff to determine the United States representative in the 1979 world team championship. The playoff lasted two days and when it was over we had lost by the slenderest of margins to the Dallas Aces, which had a reputation as the premier professional team in the country. The outcome was the equivalent to playing 72 holes of golf and getting beaten one-up. As a player, Jimmy's approach was all-business; he tried his hardest to win and he made no effort to charm. In victory, he was never especially gracious and in defeat he barely went through motions of shaking hands with the opposition. Over more than a decade, we competed in many tournaments in New York City, and our winning percentages were unbelievably high—near-total dominance. In 1981, we played in the Maccabiah Games in Israel and won the gold medal. Our successes generated publicity that occasionally referred to us as the "Greenberg team," which certainly wasn't my idea. If that bothered Jimmy, he kept it to himself.

In 1978, I offered him a chance to be co-head of private client services, our retail sales force, and a year later he became the sole head of that department. I know that some people within the firm assumed that Jimmy's upward mobility was attributable to our bridge connection. That just wasn't the case. I treated him the same way I treated other people. He constantly pushed for advancement, but I felt that signified a welcome competitiveness. My perception was based upon his results and upon how he behaved with me. He was smart and he brought in a lot of business. If he got a promotion or an increased share of the partnership's profits, those were rewards for his abilities and performance. It escaped no one that he was a political animal, but it took a long time before that characteristic seemed to me to be a liability. Jimmy and I had some great times and I thought we worked well as a team. We had dinners together, we had a lot of fun playing bridge, and I truly believed that our relationship would go on forever. But in ways small and large, that changed.

As I'VE noted, following Cy's death in 1978, the firm's growth accelerated. Within five years our retained earnings and contributions from limited partners had boosted our capital to $230 million. Our workforce had almost tripled, to 3,200, and two years later we were up to $350 million and 5,000 employees. Retail and clearing operations—we had ten branch offices and were clearing for 250 firms—accounted for a lot of this expansion and we'd begun building franchises in mortgage-backed securities and investment banking. Trading for our own account, we were consistently making big, risky but well-calculated bets on discounted bonds and undervalued equities of ostensibly troubled companies. I was as busy as ever trying to woo new customers. And, as ever, I was willing to let anyone with an idea for a new product or service have a go at it, including myself. In an attempt to invigorate our underwriting business, for instance, I spent a couple of years trying to nurture one such brainchild, a financing strategy that had never been tried.

What I had in mind was getting companies that were considering tendering for their own stock to use a Dutch auction bidding arrangement. In a typical all-vanilla tender offer, Company XYZ announces that in thirty days it intends to repurchase a million shares of its own stock at $26. If at the moment of the announcement the stock is trading at $25, a buyer could acquire shares hoping to have all the stock taken at $26, for a potential 48 percent return on an annualized basis.

Only it's rarely that simple. In some cases more than a million shares are tendered and you suffer proration; you get stuck with shares you'd anticipated cashing in for a quick profit. Or, instead of realizing a profit, you could have a paper loss if you were left with stock selling at $23 after the tender expired. At the same time, a conventional tender has some definite negatives from the company's perspective. If the stock market weakens while the tender is open, or if there's bad news about the industrial sector that the tendering company belongs in, there will probably be a huge overtender and the company will be locked into a $26 buy-in price when the stock is trading for less, even much less—a very expensive opportunity cost.

A Dutch auction tender offer works like this: Company XYZ declares that within thirty days it will buy back a million shares for an undetermined price between $23 and $26. Shareholders who tender stock name their own price (with $0.25 being the minimum allowed increment) within that spread. On the closing date, the company purchases the least expensive shares, all at the price of the millionth share tendered.

For an arbitrageur—and I guess I was wearing my old arbitrageur's hat when this notion occurred to me—the Dutch auction represented a lot more risk and usually resulted in the arbitrageur not taking a position until the last couple of days before the tender expired. For sellers, the main negative was the likelihood of getting less for their stock than in a straight tender. When I explained Dutch auctions to potential corporate clients, I stressed that management shouldn't be concerned about certain shareholders leaving the ship; their priority was to buy stock as cheaply as possible for the benefit of the other shareholders.

In a straight tender, the arb buys stock soon after the offering is announced and waits out the thirty days, probably rounding out his position along the way. Meanwhile, Company XYZ has to wait it out like a sitting duck, knowing that if any bad news emerges it will be probably be overpaying for the stock. Or, if the news is good and the market is strong, the company might not be offered any shares. The reason the arbs don't jump in early for a Dutch auction tender—holding off instead until the last day or so—is to reduce the risk that they would have paid $25 for shares that get bought at $23.

A Dutch auction, I knew, could be a win-win for the company making the tender offer. Its exotic nature, however—the concept originated in the flower trade in seventeenth-century Holland—made it automatically suspect. It had been used by city and state governments to buy in bonds when they wanted to retire their debt issues early, but that didn't stop the first couple of attorneys I ran it by from assuring me that it was unsuitable for a stock tender offer. Not that they could explain why.

I went to see Joe Flom of Skadden, Arps, the dean of mergers-and-acquisitions lawyers, and he liked the sound of it. "Call the SEC," I said—which he did, then called me back and said they wouldn't give an opinion without a test case. That launched my quest to find a company that was willing to be a guinea pig. And I couldn't. Everyone I approached blew me off. It was like trying to explain baseball's infield-fly rule to people from Borneo. The final straw, I decided, occurred during a trip I made to California specifically to see Henry Singleton, the co-founder of Teledyne, which tendered for its own stock each year. When even he didn't want to listen, I gave up. I came back to New York and said to Johnny Rosenwald, "Let's go over to Morgan Stanley and give them this." Their clients included big companies with plenty of cash, and many were in the habit of tendering for their own stock.

Johnny was a good friend of Fred Whittemore, a partner, who arranged a meeting with the head of the firm, Frank Petito. I explained my idea in depth, assuming that they would both jump all over it, but I soon got the Borneo feeling. I left there believing that we had at least gotten some honor points from Morgan Stanley, and I think they did appreciate that we came over.

Finally, in 1981, I found a taker, Todd Shipyards. They were a Bear Stearns client but in a modest way; we'd done a couple of bond issues for them. When I heard that they wanted to do a tender, my antennae shot up. And it wasn't all that difficult to persuade them to try a Dutch auction, once I had persuaded myself that getting down on my knees and begging in no way compromised my personal or professional dignity. Originally they had intended to do a straight tender for 10 percent of their common stock, 550,000 shares, at $28 apiece. The company chairman, John Gilbride, asked, "What are you going to charge us?" I said, "Nothing if you buy it for $28. If you buy it cheaper, give us a third." They ended up paying $26.50, so we got fifty cents a share and made about $250,000.

Not a stupendous profit but still a milestone; the frustration had been driving me crazy and finally I felt vindicated. When the details were reported in the *Times* and the *Wall Street Journal,* the guys from Morgan Stanley immediately called up and said, "Hey, this is what you were talking about." You can guess what happened next: Morgan Stanley and the other old-line firms started doing Dutch auction tenders themselves for their long-standing clients, and it eventually became standard operating procedure in the industry. We floated a couple more small ones but were never able to turn it into a cash cow. My idea wasn't patentable and the big firms ultimately gobbled up the big fees. Proverb debunked: being the early bird doesn't necessarily guarantee that you'll wind up with much more than hors d'oeuvres.

I don't want to give the impression that every unconventional idea I concocted met with the same resistance as the Dutch tender. In fact, some were readily accepted. For instance, I played a role forty or so years ago—toward the tail end of the fabled go-go years—in the public's embrace of stock warrants, an option derivative that gave a holder the right to buy a company's common shares at a specified price before a specified expiration date. A company that issues warrants does the same thing the U.S. Treasury does when it prints money—creates a piece of paper and declares that it has whatever value the market grants it. A warrant's exercise price (comparable to the strike price of a stock call option) always exceeds the share price of the underlying common stock.

So, for example, ABC Corporation, which trades for $10, would authorize warrants exercisable at $15, with an expiration date five years away. When that date arrives, if the stock trades for less than $15, the warrant is worthless. If at any point during those five years the stock trades at $15 or higher, ABC Corporation is obligated to give a share of stock to anyone who presents $15 and one warrant. Along the way, trading of the warrants themselves in the secondary market—where the players generally are sophisticated speculators—has waxed or waned depending upon the fluctuating price of the underlying stock. If the stock performs well, the warrant's value (its premium) represents the price per share that a holder must pay in addition to the exercise price.

Often warrants were attached to new public issues of corporate bonds, which had the effect of sweetening an otherwise staid fixed-income investment. Or else—and this was my innovation—they could be issued nakedly to existing shareholders.

In 1972, I went to see Steve Ross, the founder and CEO of Warner Communications, which had been formed by the merger of Kinney National Services, Inc., with the Warner Bros.-Seven Arts film studio and recording businesses. A decade earlier, Johnny Rosenwald and I had been instrumental in the initial public offering for Kinney, a family-owned conglomerate that included funeral homes, parking garages, rental cars, an office-cleaning business, and later a Hollywood talent agency. Steve was an entrepreneur with a habit of listening and I found him receptive to my suggestion that Warner issue stock warrants to its shareholders. "Give them ten warrants for every hundred shares," I proposed, that could be exercised within five years at 25 percent above the market at the time. "Because it's a gift, nobody will object. Your shareholders can hold them or sell them whenever they like. Meanwhile, the company can use warrants in lieu of cash to make acquisitions."

Steve loved the idea immediately. My recollection is that soon after the Warner warrants began trading in the open market, they made an offer to buy a portion of the 20th Century-Fox film library. But Fox balked.

"Why would we take these crazy things?" a Fox executive asked me.

"If you do the deal," I told him, "I assure you we'll get you out at a price that dollar-wise will make the sale palatable."

By which I meant that we were acting as underwriters of the warrants. If, say, Fox wanted $3 million out of the deal, we promised that they would get that much in the secondary market or else we would cover any shortfall. With our guarantee Fox did the transaction and with our help they soon sold the warrants for cash. Eventually Warner ran into major problems with its Atari video games division, the stock got hit hard, and the warrants became worthless. Because the warrants were never exercised, Warner had in effect bought the Fox library for nothing. The only losers were the speculators in the secondary market.

Not long after Warner embraced my advice, I got in touch with James Robinson of American Express, and laid out the concept. He asked me to appear before his board of directors and explain it to them, but as soon as I got going, the looks on their faces had me feeling that I was in Borneo with the infield-fly rule. Finally I did make the case—there was no downside, shareholders would enjoy an immediate rise in net worth, the company would give itself an expedient means of acquiring new assets, and so on—and American Express followed suit. Subsequently the broad market declined, taking with it the big premium the warrants had been selling for, but neither the company nor the shareholders got hurt. On that score, it was a win-win situation.

I mention these experiences because, frankly, they're happy memories of episodes when a brainstorm of mine proceeded smoothly and both companies gladly paid our fees without even a token effort to negotiate. Which brings me somewhat less happily to another irresistibly sensible idea of mine, slightly further afield, that has yet to gain the traction I'm convinced it deserves.

One day a few years ago, as I was watching a New York Giants football game on television, it hit me that there was a serious flaw in one of the most salient measures of a quarterback's performance: his rate of interceptions. Statistically, no one officially asks how many interceptions are truly the fault of the quarterback. So I wrote letters to the editors of both my hometown newspapers, the *New York Times* and the *Daily Oklahoman*:

> *Quarterbacks are judged by many statistics. A very important one is how many of their passes are intercepted during a season. My problem is the definition of an interception.*
>
> *If a ball bounces off a receiver's chest and is caught by the defender, should that be an interception or an error on the receiver? The same could be said for a ball that goes through the hands of a receiver and is intercepted.*
>
> *The Major League baseball season is about 162 games,*

*but for every game that is played somebody in the press box
makes a judgment on whether a ball is scored as a hit or an
error. The college football season is about 11 games and the
pros play about 16. Why isn't there someone in the press box
making a judgment on interceptions, which is so important in
evaluating the quarterback? He would probably make three
or four decisions a game. The person handling the replays
could certainly rule on who causes an interception.*

*I have discussed this with three friends of mine who own
professional teams. They don't question my logic, but for
some reason they have not pursued it with the NFL. Maybe
they are afraid it will be called the Greenberg rule and they
are jealous.*

*Where do I go from here? Is my logic wrong or is
designating a person to make the call too cumbersome?
Would love to hear your opinion.*

Truly yours,
Alan C. Greenberg.

In addition to pitching this to those NFL team owners, I
also ran it by Bob Stoops, head coach at the University of
Oklahoma. None of them has questioned my logic, but for
some reason they haven't pursued it. The newspapers didn't
even deign to publish my letters, which I take as one of the
major insults of my entire life. (Okay, I admit, it's been a
charmed life.) Anyway, if you think I was determined to get
the Dutch auction in effect for equities, I can tell you that I'm
twice as determined to have my interception-statistic inspiration accepted by somebody who has a brain.

THE INTENDED effect of my persistent admonitions to
the troops on behalf of myself and Haimchinkel Malintz

Anaynikal—a steady increase in revenue and profitability each quarter—also had the unanticipated effect of forcing us to rethink whether it made sense to remain a private partnership. Starting in the early seventies, we'd seen other Wall Street firms transform themselves into publicly owned corporations, and the larger we grew and the more businesses we ventured into, the more tempting it became for us to do the same.

When the internal discussions about going public began, I wasn't crazy about the idea. I had long been in favor of incorporating, which would allow us to limit the potential liability of each partner—in an increasingly litigious world, not a small consideration—but we could have accomplished that while remaining privately owned. Above all, I didn't want the rest of Wall Street to know how well we were doing. On the other hand, a public stock sale would allow retiring partners to cash out immediately, at the market price, with no effect upon the firm's capital, and the clear sentiment among my partners was to make the change, so I said fine. At the close of business on October 29, 1985, the first day of trading, the market price of our stock was triple the book value. Our underwriters had pushed for an offering of 10 million shares at $23 apiece. I proposed $21 because I wanted the public to get a real bargain and I wanted the stock to be favorably received by the investment community. We compromised at $21.50, and the entire issue sold out straight away. (Seven months later, in a secondary offering, the general partners—there were about one hundred of us at the time—sold 4.6 million of our shares at $35.)

In our new incarnation, general partners were called senior managing directors. At the time of the IPO each of us received an amount of stock that corresponded to our equity percentages of the partnership. Certain traditional rules and partnership rituals still applied, but now there were a lot more chips on the table. I insisted that each partner contribute to an employee stock option plan, or ESOP, which started out with $8 million. The formula for awarding those shares to individual employees was convoluted and I won't digress into the particulars, other than to say that within five years all of the stock had been disbursed, so we added another $14 million to the ESOP. In the meanwhile, we'd also had a 3-for-2 stock split; and across the years, at my instigation, we declared a consistent string of 5 percent stock dividends.

Since the mid-1960s we'd maintained a profit-sharing plan for all employees below the partnership level—not a pension fund per se but a benefit intended to enable anyone who spent the better part of a career at Bear Stearns to retire with dignity. When we funded the second ESOP, in 1990, the executive committee (consisting of between five and ten of the company's chief officers) discussed liquidating the profit-sharing plan, which was invested in diversified securities, and buying shares of Bear Stearns. This had been proposed by the company comptroller and embraced almost unanimously by the executive committee—the only naysayer being me. I never would have put all my personal eggs in one basket, and I managed my retail customers' money the same way. So there was no chance I would have exposed thousands of Bear Stearns employees to that level of risk. The vote was 8 to 1, but mine trumped all the others. Had that edict been common knowledge, I can imagine my name being taken in vain—vigorously and routinely—during the heady times when our stock traded well above $100. By the same token, when the company collapsed I doubt that it occurred to the employees enrolled in the profit-sharing plan that they had dodged at least one bullet that would have been excruciatingly painful.

At the start of every fiscal year, the corporate board of directors would provisionally allocate to the members of the executive committee a percentage of the coming year's profits to be divided among themselves. Senior managing directors, including members of the executive committee, earned an annual salary that over the years rose from $150,000 to $250,000. The executive committee took home more only if we made money. Which for the next twenty-one years—but not for twenty-two—we would accomplish. To my knowledge, no other firm on Wall Street had a strictly performance-based compensation policy for its executive committee.

Otherwise, even if the company had lost money overall or returned a small profit, individual senior managing directors and other employees received bonuses based upon their specific performance. Those deliberations fell to the company's management and compensation committee (certain executive committee members plus senior people from several departments).

From the moment of the IPO, I was afraid that the executive committee would wind up with too much of the pie, which hardly would have endeared us to the rest of our colleagues or the public, or possibly even securities analysts. Within six months my apprehensions proved well-founded. We clearly *were* on track to do too well for ourselves, and I persuaded the other committee members to reduce our percentages.

We took that same action four more times over the next twenty-one years, but it never seemed to discourage Graef Crystal, the executive compensation consultant, from consistently pouncing upon our annual report. The more profitable the year (and thus the more the executive committee members earned), the more he seemed to enjoy rubbing our noses in it.

Finally I called him to complain. "How come you never mention that our pay is based upon performance?" I asked. "We take big risks."

"There's *no* risk," he said.

"What do you mean?"

"Because you never lose money."

"What do you want us to do?" I said. "You want us to take dumb pills and lose money one year?"

"Yes," he said. "Then it would look better."

This was advice that I managed to disregard—which of course became moot the day the problem abruptly disappeared, along with Bear Stearns.

I took it for granted that all Bear Stearns employees paid close attention to our bottom line, and I wanted our profit-sharing plan, as the name implied, to spread around the spoils of success. The executive committee set the size of the annual contribution, and especially during our most lucrative years I found myself in an uphill battle with other members when I pushed to increase the profit-share contribution to our colleagues.

At one point—this was after 2001, when I had ceased being the company chairman but remained chair of the executive committee—Jimmy Cayne, then the CEO, complained, "Why are we sharing profits with all these people who probably won't be working here in five years?"

"Jimmy," I said, "a lot of these people have already been here more than ten years." Then I got busy with our personnel department to come up with a plan that rewarded em-

ployees with at least twenty-five years of service who wanted
to retire at sixty or older—an arrangement that continued to
pay them almost their full salaries after they left. I told Jimmy,
"You can't complain about giving money to people who've
shown that level of commitment."

That boxed him in, and he had to go along with it.

Jimmy's attitude didn't surprise me because it jibed with
what I'd observed almost from the day he became a partner.
As a partnership, we had a defined protocol for determining
profit shares, which we reviewed every two years. In anticipa-
tion, every partner was asked to rank himself and every other
partner on a ladder. The executive committee scrutinized the
ladder and made the final allocations. In theory, the purpose
of the rankings was to arrive at an objective performance-
based consensus, but intangibles always found their way into
the calculations. Invariably, Jimmy ranked very high. He was
a producer, by all means, in a place with a lot of producers. In
no small part, his high ranking reflected his tireless politicking. He could be charming when he wanted to—the technical
term would be kissing ass—and he certainly worked hard at
cultivating a friendship with me. Not that that ever stopped
him when the percentages were announced from complaining that I'd somehow screwed him, that I hadn't backed him
up enough, that he deserved more. He always *needed* more,
even long after, by any rational measure, he couldn't possibly
need a thing.

At first, Jimmy's avidity struck me as a mixed blessing—
according to the PSD principle, I wanted our people to be
hungry—but over time it increasingly seemed like an unfor-
tunate character trait. As head of private client services, he
pushed the retail reps out of competitive instinct and a clear
awareness that their success and the consequent rewards

would encourage a personal loyalty to him and enhance his stature. No problem with that, in principle. But in Jimmy's case that hunger for money and status, and the gamesmanship that went with it, indicated an insecurity that was no blessing at all. Jimmy was constantly caucusing and forming alliances. I didn't like it, and I told him so, but I don't think he could help himself.

I adhered to an overriding belief that my job was to ensure the steady growth and profitability of Bear Stearns. A preoccupation with power for power's sake always struck me as pointless, with no bottom-line benefit. I refused to be distracted by office politics. My priorities were making money for our partners (later for our shareholders) and enriching our employees, and, ultimately, doing whatever it took to ensure that we would be in business tomorrow.

The book *House of Cards* by William D. Cohan includes a vignette about the decision to go public, courtesy of Jimmy. As it happens, few anecdotes in that book for which Jimmy is obviously the source possess for me the ring of truth. In this instance, Jimmy described an alleged conversation that took place during our commute the morning after the executive committee voted, behind my back, to go public. It seems I'd been in Albany the day before and as we drove to 55 Water Street I asked whether anything had happened the previous evening. Jimmy purportedly said, "Not much, except we decided to go public." To which, again purportedly, I expressed complete surprise. Then he had me asking about the management structure and being informed that I would be chairman, Johnny would be vice chairman, and he would be president. This fabrication is ludicrous in every particular, starting with the fact that three of my best friends—Johnny, Alvin Einbender, and Mickey Tarnopol—sat on the executive committee and there was no way they would have allowed such a vote to be taken in my absence. None of this ever occurred. Period.

What did occur is that a few months before the IPO, I returned from a vacation and was handed a memo that referred to certain details of our offering prospectus. "Where'd this come from?" I asked. For as long as we were a partnership, we'd gotten by with very little attention paid to job titles, but the formation of Bear Stearns Companies, Inc., necessitated, on paper at least, a formal executive hierarchy. I would be the chief executive officer and Jimmy and Johnny Rosenwald would share the office of president. The memo, however, listed Jimmy as sole president, ranked a notched above Johnny, and there was no great mystery about its origins. When I asked Jimmy to explain, he said that Johnny had agreed to the change. Then I called Johnny to confirm, and he said this was the first he'd heard of it. Hmm. We went forward with the co-presidency plan.

Over the years, when various partners confided to me that Jimmy was egotistical and devious, I had little patience for anyone's complaints. For the sake of the firm, I strongly felt that personality differences had to be subordinated to our larger goals. I'm not proud of that fact—given where Jimmy's stewardship would eventually terminate. But just as no one ever truly knows how the market will behave on a given date in the future, I had no way of foreseeing that Jimmy's foibles would lead us to our ultimate destination.

8

In jimmy cayne's fanciful history of his career at Bear Stearns (as described in Cohan's *House of Cards*) one of his themes is how a pattern of shrewd and fearless power plays, often topped off by a tough-talking ultimatum, enabled him to increase his authority steadily at the expense of mine. Given my lack of psychoanalytic training, I don't pretend to know whether or not Jimmy actually believes this stuff. I will say that to the extent his versions of events depict him as unapologetically crude and bullying, they're generally accurate.

By the spring of 1988, the time seemed right to end the arrangement that had Johnny Rosenwald and Jimmy serving as co-presidents. Johnny had decided he wanted to devote more time to his philanthropic and civic commitments—he was about to become chairman of the board of trustees of both Dartmouth College and the New York University Medical Center, as well as vice chairman of the board of the Metropolitan Museum of Art—and Jimmy, of course, had chafed all along at sharing a title. So he became president and Johnny became vice chairman. Two and a half years had elapsed since our transition from a partnership to a publicly owned corporation. As a practical matter, I felt that titles still meant little, unless you were someone who enjoyed admiring yourself in the mirror while holding up your business card. I can tell you that whether you called me head of the firm or chief executive or that bald guy wearing the bowtie, I was running Bear Stearns.

Nevertheless, here's how that minor event is recounted in *House of Cards* (the sole source seems to be Jimmy): he and Johnny come to see me and explain that only one of them should be president, whereupon "Greenberg goes completely crazy. He throws his jacket on the floor." After my "tantrum," Jimmy delivers an ultimatum, "This is a fill or kill. This doesn't happen, I'm out of here. It's your firm. I don't doubt that it's your firm. But I won't be here getting coffee in the morning and the other guys' coffee in the afternoon." In response, I agree to make a formal announcement within ninety days. When the ninety days are up, I again stall, but Jimmy—again with a threat—forces me to inform the executive committee of my decision later that day, when he knows he will prevail because he already has the committee in his pocket. The meeting convenes and I announce the change offhandedly, as if I were discussing the weather: "Johnny wants to do a little something different, so he's going to move into the ivory tower, which leaves only one person in the presidency, and that's Jimmy." Then, still in weather-chat mode, I proceed to the next agenda item, which upsets Johnny, who interjects, "Well, wait a second. I've been at the firm for thirty years and I deserve a little more than simply 'John is moving into something else.' I really don't think that I was treated right." To which I respond, "Yeah, well, okay, well, so what?" The capper is a call that Jimmy says he made to Johnny at home that night because "Greenberg was a meatpacker who was treating him like a piece of dirt." And the reason for Jimmy's reaching out to Johnny—who, incidentally, is deeply moved by the gesture—is because, Jimmy later reflects, "Even though I may be rough and tough and grew up scrambling and clawing my way, there's a basic niceness and a basic humanity. I ran the firm with an idea. The idea was be nice to everybody. It works."

Where do I begin? Throwing my jacket on the floor? As anyone who ever set foot on the Bear Stearns trading floor can tell you, I spent every single workday in my shirtsleeves. I arrived in the morning, hung my jacket in a closet, put it back on for lunch, then returned it to the closet until I left at the end of the day. *Tantrum?* The whole notion is so alien to my style and temperament—I was the guy, after all, who Cy Lewis used to complain had "ice water in his veins"—that I have to marvel at Jimmy's chutzpah. Or should I say his delusional ravings? When Johnny Rosenwald read this passage he was dumbstruck. According to his memory and mine, none of what Jimmy describes ever happened—not the showdown in my office, not the scene in the executive committee meeting (the business about Jimmy having surreptitiously won over the committee is ludicrous), not the compassionate phone call. In *House of Cards*, Jimmy concedes that Johnny is "a really nice guy," but in the next breath he describes him derisively. It was well known that Jimmy resented Johnny, who is cultured, a gentleman, and a superb salesman with an effortless sense of humor. "I certainly don't remember a call from Jimmy at that time," Johnny told me. "Jimmy and I were oil and water. We almost never had a conversation about anything of consequence. Why would he call me at home? And not once in your life did you ever treat me badly."

REGARDLESS OF whatever angling and office politicking Jimmy was occupied with, for the next five years I continued to do what I'd been doing all along: chairing the executive committee, which met at least once a week; presiding at the weekly risk committee meeting; consulting constantly with our traders; dropping in on our registered reps; managing my private clients' two hundred or so discretionary accounts and executing trades for three hedge funds; being accessible to anyone (client, potential client, employee, prospective employee) who had a question or a concern; rallying the troops; being a pain in the ass about controlling costs. We were growing—in capital, net revenue, book value, volume of clearing and bond underwriting and mortgage-backed debt securitization, asset management account relationships, numbers of employees—and continuing to encourage all of our people to share their ideas for new products and improved efficiencies.

As ever, I remained skeptical of outside consultants, and though I can't prove it, my gut feeling is that my skepticism helped us avoid what might have been some costly missteps. During the merger and leveraged-buyout overenthusiasm of the 1980s and early 1990s, many of our competitors agreed to do deals that my risk calculations told me to steer clear of. One was bridge financing, a concept familiar to anyone who has ever bought a new house while trying to sell another and needs a short-term loan to cover the interval between closing dates. (Frankly, I lack firsthand knowledge in this area. I paid cash for the first apartment I bought, in 1967, and I've done the same for every piece of real estate I've since owned. So I've never actually applied for a mortgage. Nor have I personally ever used leverage. With leverage only two things can happen and one of them is bad. I've never even had a margin account. And if you asked me for the name of my personal banker I'd draw a blank.)

Would we be willing to lend to a company that needed,

say, $400 million to buy another company, with the promise that: (a) we'd be repaid with interest in six months when the borrower sold bonds, and (b) we'd get the underwriting business on the bond issue? Or would we like to take a piece of a bridge loan that another firm had originated? My answer was always the same: "We don't do bridge loans, we only do footpath loans"—a response that I'm sure often left people wondering whether they'd heard me correctly. We watched as Credit Suisse First Boston got stuck with hundreds of millions of junk bonds after financing a leveraged buyout of the Ohio Mattress Company. We were still on the sidelines when CS First Boston got walloped again, along with Paine Webber, for financing the absurdly overleveraged takeover of the Allied Stores and Federated Department Stores by the Canadian real estate developer Robert Campeau—an orgy of hubris that worked out well for none of the parties involved. What finally drew us into the game were the bargains scattered among the carcasses. Just as the firm had seized the initiative more than a half century earlier when the railroads and utilities were emerging from bankruptcy reorganization, we profited tremendously in the high-yield secondary market by trading distressed bonds that we picked up at fantastic discounts.

During this same time period, we decided in the wake of the collapse of the Soviet Union not to rush into deals with Russia's overnight capitalists. When we did do business there, we were highly selective. And even then—our participation in the 1991 privatization of Volga Auto Works comes to mind—we occasionally had trouble getting paid. From what I could gather, the new Russia resembled the old Russia, except with fewer rules and more bodyguards. Bob Strauss, the United States ambassador to Russia in the early Clinton years, begged us to set up an office in Moscow, but I told him it was too risky, too corrupt, and too many people were getting murdered there. In 1998, the Russian stock, bond, and currency markets cratered—and we didn't lose a nickel there. Whenever I was asked how we'd managed that, I said, "All of my grandparents came from Russia. They didn't really have a cheerful time there, and they made me promise never to go near the place."

Jimmy, meanwhile, continued to run private client services successfully. He also took advantage of my impatience with one particular function of the executive committee. The larger we grew, the more time-consuming the job of allocating partners' profit percentages, and I had no objection to shifting those deliberations to a compensation subcommittee, which subsequently became a separate entity comprising eight or ten senior company officers and department heads. Jimmy ran it and before long expanded its portfolio so that it was officially known as the management and compensation committee.

This change also was fine with me because the committee, which met at least once a week for three or more hours, oversaw administrative matters that I had no interest in micromanaging. In giving Jimmy that much authority, especially over compensation—a position guaranteed to help him nurture his personal alliances and broaden his influence throughout the firm—I was feeding the beast (without having gauged the beast's full appetite), but at the time I couldn't have cared less. Technically, the corporate board of directors held an ultimate veto, and the real power within the firm resided with the executive committee. Because I chaired both, it honestly didn't cross my mind that Jimmy or anyone else might usurp my authority. When Haimchinkel and I preached humility by citing the perils of "believing thine own odor is perfume," this represented practical business wisdom as well as my personal philosophy. Jimmy's need for power and the swaggering bluster that went with it—along with, as we would all discover, his need to have the largest profit share at Bear Stearns, the most lucrative compensation package on Wall Street, the biggest whatever—betrayed an insecurity that I seriously underestimated, I suppose because I'd never experienced anything like it myself. The possibility that humility could enhance one's strength and authority is something I don't think Jimmy ever pondered.

IN THE summer of 1993, Jimmy came to me with a request that caught me slightly off-guard, although, upon reflection, it shouldn't have. He was about to leave for Asia; I don't recall the specific purpose of his trip. At the time we had only a token presence there and little history. In 1990 we had opened a branch in Tokyo, with a focus on institutional fixed-income sales, mainly of American corporate bonds or securitized mortgages to Japanese pension funds, investment trusts, insurance companies, and the like. As we gradually expanded into retail brokerage and corporate finance, over the next couple of years we added a branch in Hong Kong and lightly staffed offices in Shanghai, Beijing, and Singapore.

A decade earlier we'd launched a foray into Latin America, where the currency and debt crisis presented the sort of challenge we were comfortable with—trading distressed government and corporate bonds in the secondary market—and from there we segued into underwriting and corporate finance. Asia offered an environment with richer and more diverse opportunities, but it was also a more problematic one, especially given the peculiar business protocols in China, where Westerners were trying to adjust on the fly to the vagaries of state-run capitalism. No matter what you were trying to get done in China, you learned, nothing happened quickly. There would be meeting after meeting after meeting and then, once you thought you had a deal and had signed an agreement, the Chinese would start negotiating. Despite that, competition among American and European financial institutions was intense—imagine a hundred hunters looking for two rabbits—which to me made the potential rewards seem all the more uncertain.

Jimmy's request was pure Jimmy. To cultivate business properly in Asia, he said, he needed a bigger title than president and the one he had in mind was chief executive officer. I was sixty-five and he was fifty-nine. The company didn't have a mandatory retirement age, and I hadn't given any indication that I wanted to slow down, because in fact I did not. I needed the weekend to think it over, I said, and the following Monday I gave him my decision. Yes, that could work, I told him, because I intended to remain: (a) chairman, and (b) in charge. We put out a press release stating exactly that. It should go without saying that Jimmy, via *House of Cards*, now presents a revisionist history of this event, according to which he intimidated me into submission: "If your decision is not stepping down, then, of course . . . we have war. My suggestion is just do it." Again, no such conversation took place because there's no reason why it would have. On July 14, 1993, the *New York Times* announcement of the change in Jimmy's position accurately reported the bottom line: "Mr. Cayne will take over a larger portion of the firm, but Mr. Greenberg, who continues as chairman, will remain the final authority."

I had plenty of work to do, so did Jimmy, along with everyone else at Bear Stearns, and I wasn't keeping track of his comings and goings. I knew that some of his travel to Asia coincided with international bridge competitions (including at least one invitation to a tournament in Beijing at the Great Hall of the People, in Tiananmen Square), and if I gave that any thought I saw it as a plus. On the other side of the ledger, though, were changes in the scope and cost of our activities in Hong Kong that Jimmy set in motion without bothering to consult me in advance. The goal was to establish an investment banking franchise in that part of the world, and we did participate in some IPOs that helped Chinese companies get listed on stock exchanges in both Hong Kong and New York. But these modest accomplishments were accompanied by a hiring spree that made very little sense.

Why were we paying such astronomical salaries? It was as if I'd never written a memo or certain people had never read one. If everything had gone rosily, our volume still would have had a hard time catching up with our overhead. The result was that we went from an operation that had been consistently making a moderate amount of money to one that was losing a ton. The fact that Jimmy hadn't discussed these plans with me ahead of time angered me so much that I basically stopped speaking to him for about six months. Even after that rift began to heal, a residual friction remained. Within the first couple of years over there we had dropped more than a $100 million. I was checking the profit-and-loss figures every month and he knew it.

An ominous incident that occurred shortly after Jimmy became CEO had also bothered the hell out of me. In the late summer of 1993, I attended a charity event and was seated at a table with Joseph Perella, who five years earlier, along with Bruce Wasserstein, had founded an extremely successful mergers-and-acquisitions boutique. Recently Joe had left the partnership and was in the process of deciding what to do next. As we casually discussed that, he mentioned that he'd been having hot and heavy conversations with Jimmy about joining Bear Stearns. In fact, Jimmy had taken Joe and his wife out for dinner to try to clinch the deal. This was stunning news to me, but I managed to recover immediately, knowing that Joe took it for granted that I'd been in the loop all along. Joe could have been a valuable addition to our firm, but in the end he chose to go to Morgan Stanley—depriving Jimmy, I assume, of what must have been a grandstanding fantasy of strutting into my office one day to announce that he'd landed this big fish.

Although I was tempted, I did not confront Jimmy directly. For the usual philosophical and pragmatic reasons, I saw no advantage. A war between us would have done the firm no good, and the fact was that on the whole Bear Stearns had been performing very well. As were Jimmy and I individually. In 1993, despite our voluntary decision to cut our profit share by 15 percent, we each still took home almost $16 million, thanks in large measure to outstanding results by our mortgage-backed bond trading department. Nineteen-ninety-four was better yet, likewise 1996 and 1997. The first half of 1995 proved rocky for both the bond and equity markets, which along with our Asian losses brought our earnings per share for the year down almost 40 percent. But we successfully opened our first mutual funds, and we managed the largest corporate bond offering in our history, raising $1 billion for Viacom. That piece of business, by the way, could be traced to a relationship I had developed a couple of years earlier with Sumner Redstone, the majority shareholder of National Amusements, which owns Viacom. In 1993, when Sumner was trying to buy Paramount Pictures and found himself in a bidding war with Barry Diller and John Malone, he invited me to the Four Seasons to solicit my tactical advice. I gave him a few suggestions and the following day received a check made out to Bear Stearns for $1 million, along with a note that read: "Thanks for having dinner with me." When the deal went through, he sent another $8 million, even before Bear Stearns had formally submitted a bill.

What I believe was Jimmy's most impressive achievement began to gestate in 1997, when he initiated a complex real estate negotiation that culminated five years later in our move from 245 Park Avenue to new headquarters three blocks away, at 383 Madison Avenue. We still had five years to go on our lease at 245 Park, where we'd moved from 55 Water Street a decade earlier, but there was a definite urgency in our situation. Our nonstop growth had recently forced us to add 100,000 square feet at 245 Park and we faced the prospect of needing to lease more space as well as to upgrade dramatically our electrical capacity. I preferred to stay put and fix the building, but Jimmy had a grander vision. He was right and I was wrong. He took charge and did all the negotiating with the Saudi investment group that controlled a square block near Grand Central Terminal, and then he supervised the construction of the new building. As a result, we wound up with a ninety-nine-year ground lease on a spectacular forty-seven-story (plus a five-story glass crown) state-of-the-art structure, completed on time and under budget, designed to Jimmy's specifications. It housed the largest installation of electronic and digital cable in North America and, overall, made an emphatic statement about where we were headed as a major global financial institution. After the fact there were detractors who maintained that the building was an extension of Jimmy's ego, but I thought that was beside the point. He had hit a home run, I gave him full credit at the time, and I still do.

It was that quality of positive relentlessness, combined with the rock-solid health of the firm, that made it possible for us to settle into what amounted to a functional coexistence—a coexistence that I realized would inevitably be punctuated by occasional eruptions of resentment from Jimmy.

These flare-ups tended to be amazingly petty. During the second season of the television program *The Apprentice*, in the fall of 2004, Donald Trump invited me to appear as one of four executives who evaluated the final contestants. It took some doing, but Jimmy managed to experience this as a personal affront.

As we were concluding an executive committee meeting, I asked, "Anybody have anything else?"

"Yeah, I do," said Jimmy. "You just appeared on this television show *The Apprentice*, and it's an embarrassment to the firm. You didn't discuss it with anyone ahead of time and I think it was terrible."

I said, "Jimmy, it didn't interfere with my work for Bear Stearns—it was filmed on a Sunday—and I didn't think I was doing anything wrong."

Then Warren Spector, another member of the committee, asked, "Who were the other judges?"

I mentioned the chief operating officer of Unilever, the president of Pepsi-Cola North America, and Robert Kraft, the developer and investor who owns the New England Patriots football team.

Warren said, "Bob Kraft? He's one of the best business minds in the country," which left Jimmy totally deflated. It was as if Warren and I had set this thing up, though we had not.

Even more bizarrely, Jimmy developed an irrational obsession with my nickname. I can't say exactly when it started, but word came back to me at some point that Jimmy, who always addressed me as Alan, had taken to imposing a $100 fine on anyone who referred to me as Ace in his presence. I initially thought this was a joke. Not so. What Jimmy did with the money I have no idea; if it went to charity, I'm happy that I could do my part.

As LONG as senior managing directors adhered to our tithing mandate—the "4 percent of gross income to charity" rule that I established in the early seventies—no one cared, in theory, what charities they committed to. It's true that I had no compunction about soliciting SMDs of the Hebrew persuasion to give generously to the Federation of Jewish Philanthropies. A few people resisted, which was obviously their prerogative. The sole instance I'm aware of when anyone complained about an act of philanthropy that had already occurred was in 1998, when I donated $1 million to the Hospital for Special Surgery (HSS), in New York, earmarked for Viagra prescriptions for people who couldn't afford the drug. (I intended this as a gender-neutral gift; women who qualified were also eligible.) I'd read about insurance companies and state health programs denying or limiting coverage of Viagra prescriptions because of the high cost. When some reporters asked what had prompted my donation, I kibitzed that I owned stock in Pfizer, so my motives weren't wholly altruistic.

Someone, probably in the hospital's public relations office, had tipped off the *New York Times*, which ran a story about the donation. Immediately I began hearing from friends and getting interview requests from all over the world. For a few days it was a real circus. The reaction was favorable and lighthearted, the lone dissenter being Jimmy, who didn't actually criticize me in person but behind my back whined that what I'd done was terribly undignified and damaging to Bear Stearns. Since no one else that I was aware of registered such a complaint, it became clear that what really drove him crazy was all the publicity I'd received. If you fast-forward two decades, the true reason for his indignation becomes all the more transparent. In light of the appallingly vulgar and bigoted garbage he spewed to the author of *House of Cards*—for example, his bizarrely homophobic rant about Timothy Geithner, then the president of the New York Federal Reserve Bank—who is he to make judgments about what is and isn't dignified?

Some reports about the Viagra gift mentioned that years earlier, when I paid to refurbish the bathrooms at the Israel Museum, in Jerusalem—their inspiration, not mine—wall plaques noted that my contribution had been designated in honor of my brother, Maynard. At that time, a number of people asked whether I loved or hated Maynard, a reaction I certainly hadn't seen coming. Before putting his name on the plaque I'd asked Maynard how he felt about it and he loved the idea. (When I extended the same offer to my sister, DiAnne, for reasons best known to her she declined.)

I had a great friendship with Teddy Kollek, the mayor of Jerusalem. At the time of the bathroom renovations, I became aware that he needed some cheering up; he had been deeply troubled by the Israeli occupation of southern Lebanon and was under more stress than usual. At the suggestion of the museum director, I decided to replace two of Maynard's plaques with ones identifying Teddy as the honoree. I did this knowing that he had always resisted public recognition, whether on a monument or a park bench. This specific tribute, though, he didn't object to. His thank-you letter to me said, in part:

Dear Alan:
I now know what it is to be truly honored . . . I bow my head
in deep appreciation to you—and to Maynard for giving
up not one but two of his plaques—for this unique honor.
(I am sure I have never before used the word unique with
such exactness.)
    I can only hope that my opposition does not hear of it
because I am sure they will flock to the Museum to use that
particular john, just for the pleasure of finally getting what
they feel is their due.
    In recognition of your great deeds on behalf of the
plumbing of our finest museum, I would like to present to
you the enclosed photographs of a 7th century B.C. lavatory,
excavated in the City of Jerusalem . . .
        Yours,
        Teddy

Well, that bit of frivolity put me on the radar screen of the development office at Neot Kedumim, which is described as a "Biblical landscape reserve"—an attempt to re-create the physical setting of the Bible—situated halfway between Jerusalem and Tel Aviv. Neot Kedumim wrote me a letter saying they'd heard about my gift to the Israel Museum, assumed I must have been raised on a farm with no plumbing, and could use twenty new bathrooms themselves. No problem, I said, then discovered that my sister had changed her mind and now just about everybody else in the family wanted one dedicated in his or her honor, too—my son, my daughter, several cousins, even my Lutheran mother-in-law from Minnesota. That added up.

ANOTHER PROJECT in Israel that got gratifyingly out of hand was located in Har Gilo, on the southern outskirts of Jerusalem. In this case Teddy Kollek was the instigator, having asked whether I'd be willing to help build a badly needed junior high school.

If I'd put up half the money, the government would put up the rest, which seemed like a good deal to me, especially because I got to name it for my mother in time for her eightieth birthday. (It turned out she had another eighteen years left in the tank.) I think of it as the best charitable investment I ever made because as the population of Har Gilo mushroomed, the deal got better and better. The government kept building new additions to Esther Greenberg Junior High School until it looked as if I'd endowed something the size of Ohio State University. Naturally, Teddy knew the score, and he came back to me and explained that anyone in Har Gilo who felt like swimming had to travel almost forty miles to the Mediterranean. That's how the Ted Greenberg Sports Center, which was named after my father and included an Olympic-sized pool, materialized adjacent to the school. A few years later they hit me up again because they needed a kiddie pool to divert small children who'd been peeing in the big pool. Apparently those tykes had some intuition about my history of lavatory philanthropy. Finally, I was asked to underwrite a senior center where folks could knit and play cards and schmooze. By then they'd run out of space, so the senior center had to be built underground (causing me to wonder whether that might have been interpreted as a rather mixed message).

That gift to the Hospital for Special Surgery, as it happened, was redeployed. More enlightened reimbursement rules by medical insurers had made my crusade to combat Viagra sticker shock a less urgent priority. My wife, Kathy, and I consulted Dr. Stephen Paget, the physician-in-chief of the department of rheumatology and an exemplary human being, and the result was the Greenberg Academy for Successful Aging program. As a nouveau septuagenarian, I arguably had a vested interest in gerontological issues. Kathy has served as a trustee of the hospital since 1993 and it has been one of our favorite philanthropic causes, along with the New York Public Library, the American Museum of Natural History, New York University, and my alma maters the University of Oklahoma and the University of Missouri. In 2003 we made a major new gift to HSS, endowing the Kathryn O. and Alan C. Greenberg Center for Skeletal Dysplasias. Dysplasia is the category for a wide variety of congenital disorders that manifest themselves as bone and cartilage malformations, dwarfism being the most common.

The Little People of America, which is the best-known advocacy organization for people with dwarfism, has had me in its Rolodex for decades. My interest in this subject began inadvertently about fifty years ago, when I saw a newspaper story about a young girl who had been operated on at the Johns Hopkins Hospital in Baltimore to correct complications of dwarfism. I sent Johns Hopkins a check for $100 and asked that they buy the girl some toys. The next thing I knew I had a visit from Kay Smith, who did development work on behalf of Dr. Victor McKusick, a world-class geneticist at Hopkins. "You have to understand," she said, "people will give money for puppies or whales or porpoises, but they won't give for little people." After that, Kay would call me on a case-by-case basis when a patient needed help, and this eventually led to the creation of the Greenberg Center for Skeletal Dysplasias at Johns Hopkins Hospital. Over the years I kept hearing from little people in the New York City area who said they didn't have the money to go to Baltimore routinely. So I proposed to HSS the creation of a similar research and treatment facility and they took the ball and ran with it. When I once spoke at a dinner at Johns Hopkins, I told about my first encounter with Kay Smith so long ago. "The moral of this," I said, "is never let anyone come in person to thank you."

The fact is that I consider my gifts to have been modest compared to the generosity of many people. And you can probably gather that I am certain anyone can derive a profound satisfaction from the act of giving itself. Quite simply, Kathy and I have reaped a tremendous amount of joy from this aspect of our life. Ultimately, it's been a gift to ourselves.

NOT LONG ago I was looking through some Bear Stearns annual reports. In one "Letter to Shareholders" I spied the phrase "near meltdown in worldwide financial markets" and did a double-take—a reflexive "So you think *that* was a meltdown." The "you" in question, needless to say, was yours truly. I had signed the letter in my capacity as chairman of the board. So had Jimmy, as president and CEO. That same page featured side-by-side photographs of each of us smiling contentedly. The annual report told the tale of fiscal year 1999 and the mention of a close brush with the apocalypse referred to events of the late summer of 1998, when the devaluation of the ruble and Russia's default on its International Monetary Fund and World Bank loans unleashed a panic that destabilized debt and equity values globally. As I noted earlier, our exposure in Russia was minimal, but no one and no market was completely insulated from the fallout.

Inevitably in such situations, the classic flight to safety ensues, a dash for the exits as investors take whatever losses they can sustain, or profits they've been riding, and convert securities to cash. Suddenly everyone's a seller, arbitrage spreads widen, and whether you're an individual or an institution, the more your holdings are leveraged, that is, borrowed, the more prone you are to the sensation that your entire life is flashing before your eyes.

Since 1994, Bear Stearns had been clearing trades—a huge volume on a daily basis—for Long-Term Capital Management (LTCM), a hedge fund that at its peak held more than $100 billion in assets, with a leverage ratio that at times ran as high as 50 to 1. The credit facilities that made this sort of leverage possible had been provided by the crème de la Wall Street, institutions willing to bank on the track record of John Meriwether, LTCM's cofounder. Meriwether had had a storied and on the whole laudable career running the arbitrage and bond trading departments at Salomon Brothers— this despite, in my estimation, his irrational devotion to a strategy of riding losses until they turned into gains. In the book *When Genius Failed*, a saga of the mercurial history of LTCM, Roger Lowenstein writes of Meriwether's "deceptively simple" solution to the challenge of how to gain a competitive edge that would yield a superior trading advantage: "Why not hire traders who were *smarter?*" My own succinct history of Long-Term Capital goes like this: It was a spectacularly successful money machine. Until it wasn't.

A brain trust of economists (including two Nobel laureates) and mathematicians had developed LTCM's dauntingly complex trading model, which was predicated upon—I'm oversimplifying—exploiting temporary disparities between the market prices of derivatives (such as options and credit swaps) and their underlying securities. During its first two years, investors, who were far outnumbered by those who had been turned away, enjoyed returns of around 40 percent. (Jimmy, among the privileged few, invested $10 million of his own money.)

Then the 1998 panic and flight to safety occurred, LTCM's capital began to vaporize, and its lenders began to panic themselves. If LTCM failed, these lenders—which included Bankers Trust, Chase Manhattan, Merrill Lynch, Morgan Stanley, Lehman Brothers, J.P. Morgan, and Salomon Smith Barney—potentially stood to lose hundreds of millions of dollars. As LTCM's clearing agent, Bear Stearns was in a uniquely hazardous position. Our risk consisted of the overnight credit, hundreds of millions at a given moment, that we extended between the date of a trade and its settlement. For weeks, I chaired almost daily meetings of the executive committee that were consumed with the LTCM tailspin. The climactic episode of the crisis was an emergency gathering of the heads of sixteen major banks on September 23, 1998, at the New York Federal Reserve Bank. The meeting's stated agenda was momentous: avert the imminent collapse of LTCM, buy time for an orderly liquidation, and in the process prevent the entire banking system from taking a swan dive into an empty pool. (This was a hypothesis, understand, that the Bear Stearns executive committee never bought into. Whatever the individual exposure of LTCM's lenders, we felt that each of them was solid enough to absorb its losses.)

At the beginning of 1998, LTCM's capital had exceeded $4.5 billion, but by the third week of August it stood at $2 billion. It continued to deteriorate as equity prices fell, fears multiplied, and capital fled to Treasury bills, gold, and Grandma's mattress. Meriwether and his partners were desperate for fresh capital. By September 23, LTCM had only $500 million in cash, and a large burp from the market could have wiped that out in a single day.

Merrill Lynch had proposed a rescue by the sixteen firms represented at the Fed summit, a commitment of $250 million apiece that would raise $4 billion. However, Bear Stearns was literally having none of it. In my mind, and this opinion was shared unanimously by our executive committee, the $500 million balance of LTCM's unsettled trades was the sum of our risk tolerance, our absolute limit. I chose not to attend the meeting at the Fed. Our delegates would be Jimmy and Warren Spector, an executive vice president in charge of all fixed-income trading except for municipal bonds and also a member of both the executive and management and compensation committees. My instructions to them couldn't have been simpler: "You're going to walk into that room, they're going to ask for money, and we're not going to provide it. Our overriding responsibility is to take care of the goose that keeps laying our golden eggs. We're running enough risk every day. Tell whoever's running the meeting not to poll the banks in the room alphabetically. That way someone else might announce that they're not investing either before we have to. But no matter what, we're not going to risk the franchise."

Jimmy stuck to the script. When he declared that Bear Stearns would not invest $250 million in Long-Term, would not invest a *nickel*, there was a moment of incredulous silence followed by an eruption of outrage. The meeting halted and Jimmy and Warren retreated to an adjacent room, where they were soon joined by David Komansky, the chairman of Merrill Lynch, whose first words were "What the *fuck* are you doing?" Once he settled down, they agreed upon an improvised script, and when the meeting resumed they followed it. Komansky vouched for Bear Stearns's integrity and Jimmy stated that as LTCM's clearing agent we had no special knowledge of previously undisclosed difficulties with the hedge fund; they were in compliance with their original clearing agreement. But Bear Stearns would not budge on the $250 million ante. That afternoon I got a call from Sandy Weill, the chairman of Salomon Smith Barney (and later of Citicorp), during which he tried to pressure me into changing our vote. I reiterated our one-word answer.

Officials at the Federal Reserve Bank, to their credit, never once hinted that we should reconsider. Ultimately, the other banks at the table came up with $3.65 billion, all of which they got back after LTCM was liquidated. Meriwether and Long-Term's other investors lost their entire stake, which at the beginning of 1998 had stood at $1.9 billion. Ten million of that, as I said, had been Jimmy's.

A decade later, after Bear Stearns had completed in its own death spiral, there were repeated assertions in the press that our conduct during the LTCM debacle was partly to blame. In other words, in some twisted formulation we were simultaneously architects of our own doom and victims of retribution for our unwillingness to play ball—vengeance with overkill. Jimmy, who by 2008 had been both CEO and chairman for seven years, was singled out as the culprit. In spite of our differences, he and I both recognized the ridiculousness of this analysis. In Warren Buffett's office in Omaha there's a framed letter confirming that Berkshire Hathaway, Goldman Sachs, and American International Group (AIG) were prepared to buy LTCM for $250 million and invest an additional $4 billion to keep it securely afloat. Whatever Bear Stearns was or wasn't willing to do never jeopardized the rescue, much less the banking system as a whole. The suggestion that ten years later these same firms had satisfied a grudge that had been festering through multiple management turnovers was utter nonsense. Still, if there's blame to assign to anyone at Bear Stearns, I accept with pleasure. Any heat Jimmy had to take for that he didn't deserve.

Memories of turbulent events are so often selective or unrecognizably distorted. Never mind anyone else's impression at the time or at present, our role in the LTCM crisis played out as it did because I called the shots. Three years after those events, though, I was ready for a formal transfer of authority. An official announcement took place June 26, 2001. I was seventy-three. When I first told Jimmy I wanted to retire, he tried to dissuade me, not out of any love or loyalty but because he wasn't yet ready to make certain decisions about who would be anointed as *his* likely successor. The two leading candidates were Warren Spector and Alan Schwartz, who was the head of investment banking. I suggested to Jimmy that he name them co-presidents and co-chief operating officers and that I would become chair of the executive committee. After vacillating for two or three months, he agreed.

Meanwhile, in stepping aside at a moment of my own choosing I was fulfilling a plan that I'd contemplated for a long while. No one had pushed me and nothing was stopping me. I wanted to emulate the leave-takings of certain other people whom I greatly admired—Beverly Sills, Senator Abe Ribicoff, and dozens of professional athletes who chose to leave the game while still in their prime. So that's what I did.

9

THE DAY I STOPPED BEING CHAIRMAN of Bear Stearns Companies, Inc., I also stopped writing memos. I had done what I could to infuse particular habits of mind into our DNA. Now that Jimmy was the boss, I did not intend to cross certain lines. We employed 10,500 people. We operated thirty businesses, and I would never have pretended to be familiar with the ins and outs of most of them. My sense of my role as a member of the executive and risk commit- tees remained the same; I said what I thought, as forcefully as necessary, and let the chips fall. Executive committee votes often weren't unanimous and I wasn't always in the majority, but our discussions were candid and to the point. On the risk committee, only two votes mattered—Warren Spector's and my own—and the protocol was cut and dried; either we were too long or too short or just about right. My daily presence on the trading floor, I felt, made a statement that was neither blunt nor subtle: as long as I'm still working here, we're not going to be doing dumb stuff. My phone still rang seventy or a hundred times a day.

For the next five or six years most things continued to get better. Between 2001 and 2006, our earnings per share almost quadrupled, net revenue increased by more than $4 billion, our book value reached $86 per share, and our stock price reflected that. A major proportion of our profits now came from the fixed-income division—trading gains on corporate and municipal bonds, commissions, appreciation in the value of our own portfolio, and fees generated by newly developed products, especially derivatives. All of this fell within Warren's purview, as did Bear Stearns Asset Management, which operated a diverse selection of hedge funds that catered to high-net-worth individuals. As time went by, Warren also began to assume oversight of equity trading, which historically had been my turf. That incursion began when, without consulting me, he raised position limits on some of our arbitrage trading. I didn't appreciate the way he went about it but, as in my dealings with Jimmy, I didn't pick a fight. The fact was that I had a lot of respect for Warren's abilities and there was no point in rocking a ship that was sailing as smoothly as ours.

I had a similar high regard for Warren's co-president, Alan Schwartz. In discussions with my wife, when I referred to the firm's ruling triumvirate I had a nickname for each: Ego, Smarts, and Smoothie.

Ego obviously was Jimmy, a self-important tough talker whose listening skills diminished in inverse proportion to our stock price and the number of shares he owned. Basically, from the moment Jimmy became chairman, he made no pretense of concealing his disdain for my ideas or opinions. Several months after the transition, I read about Sherron Watkins, the Enron vice president who first blew the whistle on that colossal fraud by informing Kenneth Lay, the CEO, of misstatements in financial reports. I thought we should offer her a spot on the board of Bear Stearns. This would have sent a valuable message to our own people and to the outside world. Jimmy dismissed it out of hand.

"Don't you even want to interview her?" I asked.

No, he emphatically did not. End of discussion.

The monikers I chose for Warren and Alan were not at all pejorative.

Warren was Smarts and I think anyone who observed him close up would consider that apt. He had a superior mathematical aptitude that he combined with an intuitive feel for trading and the laws of probability, which translated into prodigious profits for Bear Stearns and a compensation package for himself that by 1996 was second only to Jimmy's. If the first thing Warren's colleagues noticed about him was his intellect, often the next was his lack of humility. More than once I heard him described as someone who would ask your opinion and tell you what it was before you answered.

Whether or not Warren harbored any self-doubts, he exuded self-confidence. He definitely made a positive initial impression upon me—at least he says he did, and I take his word for it. Years after he joined the firm, he mentioned that I had hired him. Never mind that I couldn't recall having done so; I hired hundreds of people. According to Warren, while he was still in business school he wrote to me asking about a job and followed up with a phone call. I told him to come in for an interview and then passed his letter on to someone else, having already given my blessing. Evidently I didn't hold his résumé against him; he had an MBA from the University of Chicago and he'd been an undergraduate at Princeton before transferring to St. John's College in Annapolis, Maryland, where the curriculum is devoted to the Great Books. I don't think Warren often found himself in conversations with other traders about the Peloponnesian War or *The Divine Comedy*. When he was eighteen years old he had won the title of Scholastic King of Bridge, a designation conferred by the American Contract Bridge League upon the best high school–age player in the country. During our telephone interview, he kept that to himself. Nor did he ever volunteer it; Jimmy stumbled across that information after Warren had been at the firm for several years. In any case, his bridge exploits had no bearing upon his upward mobility. When he came to work for us he was immediately assigned to the fixed-income division, and in one capacity or another he spent his entire career there. His abilities were quickly noticed, he became a trader specializing in mortgage-backed bonds, and four years later he was made a senior managing director. He joined the management committee in 1990 and the executive committee in 1992, when he was thirty-four. In 1996, the first time he took home more than I did, he earned $19 million.

I have a clearer recollection of Alan Schwartz's early days at Bear Stearns, and I distinctly do remember hiring him. In his own way he was every bit as self-possessed as Warren, but without the cockiness. He was an excellent athlete, tall and lean, and had attended Duke University on a baseball scholarship. He had a 95 mile-per-hour fastball and might well have made it to the major leagues—the Cincinnati Reds drafted him after his junior year—if he hadn't developed arm trouble. By the time he graduated, he'd made peace with the fact that his career alternatives lay elsewhere. He started out in institutional sales and came to Bear Stearns four years later, in 1976. I talked him into working in our Dallas office. Then, when he'd been there only a few months, I asked him to return to New York to run our research department. It felt strange making that request. Alan was happy in Dallas—the OPEC-driven oil boom was on, which meant lots of potential clients, and he had a girlfriend there—but he was a quintessential team player and he agreed. Strategically, I believed it was the right thing to do for Alan and for Bear Stearns.

For about a month Alan stayed in my apartment while looking for a place of his own. It didn't take long for him to vindicate my instinct that he would turn around the research department. He hired additional analysts and basically made our research a more sophisticated and valuable product. Along with Lawrence Kudlow, the economist, he made presentations to institutions all over the country that proved to be a very effective sales tool. In the mid-eighties he decided he wanted to shift to corporate finance—following the same career progression Jerry Kohlberg had a generation earlier, as it happened—because he felt he could build upon his research background by pursuing mergers-and-acquisitions business in industries that he'd been following closely for years. Alan turned out to be absolutely right about that. Our M&A group never achieved the heavyweight status of major players like Goldman Sachs, First Boston, and Lazard, but under his leadership we developed a solid reputation and a lucrative franchise doing advisory work. In 1989, he joined the executive committee.

My experience with Alan was that everything he was asked to do, he did well, with a diplomatic finesse. If any friction subsequently arose between Alan and Warren in their capacity as co-chief operating officers, I was never aware of it. Working in different areas of the firm reduced the potential for turf battles, as did the fact that each was secure and comfortable in his own skin. In the best sense, each minded his own business, and they had in common an accumulated understanding of the most successful strategies for handling Jimmy. (Though the day would come when the relationship between Jimmy and Warren would become flat-out antagonistic.)

• • •

IN GOOD times or bad, money is always looking for a happy home. Or, more to the point, a happier home. Anyone with a dollar to invest wants to receive the highest possible return within his tolerable limits of risk. Depending upon the investor, over time that tolerance might very well fluctuate. The history of financial booms and busts is a continuous narrative loop in which the laws of gravity are magically suspended until, like a roller coaster that's momentarily crested, they vengefully kick back in. What amazes me more than any spectacle of boom-and-bust is our capacity as a species to witness speculative bubbles inflating and bursting—or, to have read about the most notorious case studies, such as tulipomania or the South Sea Bubble—and yet fail to remember the inevitable outcomes. How do habitually cautious investors lose their bearings and forget what their risk tolerance is? Greed deserves most of the credit, and when I say that I make no moral judgments. Not about everyday greed, anyway—never to be confused with the greed that leads to criminality—because I believe it's an innate appetite. Charles Darwin figured this out. A five-year-old boy (or a grown man) can possess a very large assortment of marbles, many more than he can play with at any one time, and if the opportunity arises to acquire a few more without going to much trouble, he's definitely interested. Someone earning an enviable 9 percent steady return is invariably willing to fantasize about 10 percent.

The direct antecedent of the subprime mortgage madness was the dot-com silliness of the 1990s. Bear Stearns had a front-row seat at a pivotal moment in that era—the November 1998 initial public offering of theGlobe.com, a social networking website that expanded into computer gaming. We were the underwriter on the IPO, which took place as the company's registration statement was about to expire. When we put out the word that we were going to do the deal, orders started flowing in. We thought $9 a share was a reasonable target—but not $87, its opening price the first day, and not $63.50, where it closed. This price set a record for history's largest opening day price rise of an IPO. At one point the bid had actually hit $97. The last I heard of theGlobe.com, it was trading for ten cents.

For my part, there was never a question about Bear Stearns holding on to these new issues for our own account. We underwrote them, we sold them, but they immediately sold in the aftermarket for such high prices that I personally never owned this stuff, nor did any of my accounts keep them. In the spring of 2000, when I spoke at the TED (Technology, Entertainment, Design) conference in California, I said that the dot-com stock prices reminded me of tulipomania. At the offering price, these were a fair value, but the multiples they sold at subsequently were ridiculous. Kathy attended with me and afterwards told me, "Don't say that anymore. They're going up 10 percent a day. Maybe you don't understand the new world of technology." So I stopped, and then when dot-com stocks started collapsing, as all along I had strongly suspected they would, she said, "Okay, you can talk about them now."

The funding for dot-com start-ups almost always came from venture capitalists, and an IPO always signified that the amateurs were entering the game. Individual bubbles merged into one colossal bubble. Hundreds of billions of dollars of market capitalization (aka "wealth") vanished, but elsewhere on Earth trillions of dollars of cash reserves remained. A lot of it accumulated in the major oil-exporting countries and a lot in China, India, and other newly industrializing or modernizing economies, especially in Asia, where cheap labor and other costs made it possible to produce and sell more goods

much more competitively than American manufacturers
could. Institutional investors here began stocking their portfolios with international equity fund shares. Then, as the U.S.
economy started to recover, helped along by monetary policies that kept interest rates low, the amateurs and pros alike
reconnected with their speculative impulses and decided that
real estate literally and figuratively could provide a new happier home for their money.

In the early 1980s a new financial product had appeared
called the mortgage-backed security. Its function was to enable banks, savings-and-loans, and other mortgage lenders
to generate business more quickly without assuming significantly greater risks. Instead of holding on to mortgages until
the borrowers had repaid them, lenders sold these assets, usually at face value, pocketed ample loan-origination fees, and
agreed to continue servicing the loans (collecting interest and
principal repayments) while simultaneously hunting for fresh
borrowers. The loan buyers, or parties higher up on the food
chain to whom *they* subsequently sold the loans—eventually,
investment banks—in turn "bundled" the loans, divided them
into affordable-enough units of debt securities that promised
a fixed rate of return, slapped their own reputable name-
brand labels on each new issue, and sold the hell out of them
to institutions and high-net-worth individuals. (The cou-
pons on these securities depended upon the perceived riski-
ness of the underlying mortgage-backed assets; the yields on
all of them, naturally, were lower than the initial borrowers
had agreed to pay.) Lubricating this process were the credit-
rating agencies, which in theory had rigorously scrutinized
and evaluated the new issues. The original mortgage-backed
securities were a relatively innocuous commodity that over
time evolved into more elaborate products, many of which—

e.g., variegated collateralized debt obligations—are now widely deemed toxically sinister.

In 1983 Bear Stearns began issuing and trading mortgage-backed bonds, including a $1.5 billion issue that was then the largest corporate debt sale in history. Seismic changes occurred between then and late 2005–early 2006, when evidence emerged that the real estate bubble had begun to deflate. In this particular game the amateurs were new home buyers or existing homeowners or, in some cases, cottage-industry speculators, all of whom had been pleasantly surprised to learn, starting around 2002 or 2003, that it wasn't nearly as hard to get a mortgage or a home-equity loan as they had always assumed. Thus did trillions of dollars of mortgage loans get booked, much of it borrowed by people who, whether or not they understand it to this day, had been in over their heads from the get-go. For millions of Americans who had never before seriously believed that they might own a house, or a bigger house than the one they were living in, this abrupt discovery in a deflating real estate market meant that the happier home dream hadn't turned out to be happier after all.

During the intervening two-plus decades, Bear Stearns stood front and center in the mortgage-backed securities business. We ranked number one in 1989 and from year to year we remained in the top handful of securitization underwriters. In 2002 we were number two, and the following year *Fortune* named us the second most admired securities firm on Wall Street, a tribute to our having avoided the common pitfalls of the dot-com excesses as well as our having sustained a terrifically profitable fixed-income business. The year after that, *Fortune* upgraded us to *the* most admired. As the party was about to end, our 2006 annual report noted: "Bear Stearns's mortgage franchise continues to lead the industry.

We ranked number one for the third consecutive year in U.S. mortgage-backed securities underwriting ... Our vertically integrated mortgage franchise allows us access to every step of the mortgage process, including origination, securitization, distribution, and servicing."

Housing prices and the rate of new construction had already begun to slide. Borrowers, especially subprime borrowers with adjustable-rate mortgages, were defaulting in numbers that could not be ignored, even though many investors still seemed almost willfully not to notice. Our stock price didn't peak until January 17, 2007, at $172.69.

As I've already indicated, I'm basically allergic to leverage. I avoid it personally, and although I recognize that our industry could not function without it, I apply the same cold-eyed standard when defining what qualifies as a tolerable leverage ratio as I do when deciding whether a given position amounts to overexposure. During risk committee meetings, whenever it was reported that any mortgage-backed securities had stayed on our books longer than ninety days, I said, "Just sell them." At such moments, I almost never encountered resistance from Warren. But as the housing bubble inflated, the dynamic shifted. For starters, it's important to take into account that the run-up in real estate prices wasn't originally perceived as a bubble. And when such apprehensions did begin to surface, they were neutralized by a chronic wishful optimism, an outlook colored by the tremendous success of our fixed-income division. Without leverage, it would have been impossible for us, or anyone else, to accumulate the debt assets that we then so lucratively securitized. Under the circumstances, on occasions when I voiced my customary skepticism I didn't really have a chorus backing me up.

The only thing I could do, I felt, was to keep things honest by asking pointed questions about individual positions and broader questions about what sorts of hedges we had in place to limit the downside if the prevailing optimism turned out to be misguided. Otherwise, I trusted Warren's track record and I also took at face value the ratings on the bonds that we bought, traded, underwrote, held, or issued ourselves. When our most experienced traders surveyed the marketplace and decided to acquire bundles of pooled mortgages rated AAA, we could confidently assume that AAA meant what it always had—borrowers who were safe, stable, reliable, eminently bankable . . . right? Nor had the definitions of AA or A changed, the ratings on bundles we also went after, knowing that in the buoyant atmosphere of the real estate boom our buyers had become more risk-tolerant. (Mind you, this occurred long before we learned that the ratings agencies, themselves infected with irrational exuberance, may have compromised their own standards to accommodate the companies that hired them.) The ultimate reason our bankers were willing to loan thirty or forty dollars for every dollar of capital we exposed was because we were Bear Stearns, we managed risk, we had a blue-chip balance sheet of our own, we knew our business.

IN THE late spring of 2007, I started hearing about a serious problem within Bear Stearns Asset Management (BSAM), our division that operated a dozen or so hedge funds. Each fund had a specific investment strategy and asset base—equities (long, short, market-neutral, domestic, international, health care, distressed stocks) and fixed-income (asset-backed, mortgage-backed, derivatives, and other esoteric stuff). Some were definitely riskier than others, and their prospectuses spelled that out. What the funds had in common, beyond the

Bear Stearns imprimatur, was the goal of helping our richest clients get richer. Historically, our shareholders also made out pretty well; a typical fund charged an annual management fee of 2 percent and retained 20 percent of the profit.

One of the notable success stories, the High-Grade Structured Credit Strategies Master Fund, opened in October 2003, and specialized in highly rated mortgage-backed securities. It was capitalized with $800 million—only $20 million of it the firm's money, an investment authorized by Warren—and managed by Ralph Cioffi and Matthew Tannin. I didn't know Tannin, but Cioffi had been with us for over twenty years. He was smart, energetic, and well-liked, with a reputation as a killer salesman. The investors included institutions and individuals, among the latter a large number of Bear Stearns employees. Cioffi and Tannin also personally invested. For the better part of three years, everyone associated with the fund was happy—investors, banks that financed the acquisition of the fund's assets, and the banks and other institutions that supplied those assets. The fund returned almost 19 percent during its first full year and over a three-year period averaged around 12.5 percent annually. Those results fed what, in retrospect, amounted to a textbook example of the overconfidence that Haimchinkel Malintz Anaynikal had so tirelessly cautioned against.

Exhibit A was the High-Grade Structured Credit Strategies Enhanced Leverage Fund, the spawn of the first fund. "Enhanced leverage" indicated that a higher percentage of borrowed capital was deployed, with the potential to yield a higher rate of return for investors who were willing to tolerate a corresponding increase in risk. For the strategy to work, the market in mortgage-backed assets had to remain fluid and the fund assets had to stay in motion. Like its precursor, it

139

was launched with about $550 million in capital from some of our best clients, all of whom presumably understood that this was not an opportunity for the faint of heart—no widows, orphans, or novices. It officially opened for business in August 2006.

Within the Bear Stearns corporate organization, the hedge funds were walled off from our everyday trading operations. Our clients' money, but very little of our own, was on the line, so the inventories of hedge fund portfolios never qualified as an agenda topic for the risk committee. Instead, I became aware that a crisis existed only when the executive committee got involved, and by then it was quite late in the proceedings. Whether it was a domino effect or a vicious circle (choose your metaphor), the root of the trouble was an accelerating rate of defaults by individual home buyers—mom-and-pop mortgage borrowers who simply had no hope of meeting their monthly interest payments. Which led to: reduced cash flow into the funds, reduced collateral, margin calls and demands from lenders for additional collateral, an urgency to sell assets that by definition made them more difficult to sell in a marketplace depressed by an oversupply of securitized debt and an alarming scarcity of buyers . . . triggering further depletion of collateral and a backlog of requests for redemptions from investors . . . which further taxed liquidity until finally, on June 7, 2007, the Enhanced Fund announced that it would suspend redemptions. A few weeks later the High-Grade Fund did likewise. As of June 30, the unavoidable conclusion was that both funds were in need of a white knight and the only plausible candidate was Bear Stearns Companies, Inc. Realistically, no matter how this played out, investors would recover, at best, a fraction of their equity, with a rash of lawsuits more than likely to follow.

By mid-June, the executive committee was meeting twice a day, sessions often attended by key employees from the trading and asset-management divisions. The most memorable and most fateful of these was a June 19 joint meeting of the executive and management-and-compensation committees. At the outset, Jimmy asked for a clarification of the amount of our exposure to the funds. Beyond the $20 million initial investment, it seemed that the figure had grown to $45 million. Where did the additional $25 million come from? Warren answered the question: "I did it. I fucked up."

I couldn't believe what I was hearing and clearly Jimmy couldn't either. Seven weeks earlier, without consulting the executive committee, Warren had unilaterally and inexcusably decided to kick in $25 million of shareholders' money. His logic—that in the face of mounting redemption requests this contribution would affirm Bear Stearns's general commitment while helping to keep the funds liquid—was, to be generous, suspect. The market just as readily could have interpreted that move as a sign of anxiety on our part, which is more or less what happened. Redemption requests accelerated and blew through the $25 million within a few days. By mid-June the situation had deteriorated drastically and the debate within the executive committee amounted to a grim calculation: what would be the cost—and by what measures would it be worthwhile—for the firm to take our bankers off the hook by replacing them as the principal lender to the funds?

If we didn't do it, whoever lost money—investors, lenders—would be extremely unhappy and litigation would follow. And even if we did, it was impossible to make everyone whole, so litigation was a certainty no matter what. My viewpoint, I know, struck some people as quaint or sentimental. For the same basic reasons that we had sustained a sterling credit rating for decades—because we stood behind our products, put our money behind our name, recognized our obligations to our clients, and planned to be in business tomorrow—I believed we were duty-bound to intervene. The counterargument was that everybody was a grown-up and the risks were well understood. The executive committee vote was as close as it could be: Jimmy and Sam Molinaro, our chief financial officer, took the hard line, but Warren and Alan Schwartz agreed with me that we couldn't just walk away and leave our bankers and clients holding the bag.

Two days later, an official announcement went out: we were willing to lend up to $3.2 billion to enable the High-Grade Fund to unwind in an orderly fashion. In the opinion of people I had confidence in, there was $400 million of equity left, and if the liquidation was allowed to proceed carefully— because, for a change, the fund's lenders weren't breathing fire—investors would get some of their money back. The Enhanced Fund, however, was doomed by its inventory of collateralized debt obligations and overexposure to the subprime mortgage market; no projected equity remained and there was nothing we could do about it.

Bear in mind that the funds' net asset values were a moving target, and it soon became apparent that our rescue strategy for the High-Grade Fund had failed. By selling what we could of the fund's assets, within a week we had reduced our exposure as repo lender to $1.6 billion. The remaining collateral turned out to be worth far less than we'd calculated, and the prediction that the High-Grade Fund still had $400 million of remaining equity was illusory. By the time the liquidation was completed, the price tag on the firm's loss came to almost

$1 billion. Knowing what I knew at the time, I thought we had done the proper and honorable thing.

This debacle would soon evolve into a full-blown melodrama within the firm. Our balance sheet remained strong and our liquidity hadn't been visibly strained. But, suddenly, being Bear Stearns no longer automatically entitled us to the benefit of the doubt. Rather than being perceived as proof of our strong capital and liquidity, bailing out the hedge funds was read by many as a sign of weakness and insecurity. Once bad news accumulates, more tends to follow. A cascade loomed on the horizon. None of us yet recognized it as such, but the demise of Bear Stearns had inexorably been set in motion.

CHAPTER

10

IN SEPTEMBER OF 2007 I TURNED
eighty. Despite my abiding gratitude for my many blessings,
I wasn't much enjoying myself. Largely as a result of our
hedge fund fiasco, over the summer the atmosphere in the
office, particularly where Jimmy Cayne and Warren Spector were concerned, had become disturbingly fractious. The
fixed-income markets had turned against us, most acutely
in our mortgage-backed holdings. For some time I'd found
myself during meetings of the executive committee listening
to strategic proposals that made less and less sense to me.
In October, I learned that I had prostate cancer and began
radiation treatment—an unwelcome turn of events that had
to assume its place in line along with the other ill tidings.
By very unlucky coincidence, several months earlier my son,
Teddy, had received an identical diagnosis. (Thankfully, Teddy
fully recovered and is now fine. As am I.) None of this, to put
it mildly, was what I had in mind. So it wasn't as if I arrived
at 383 Madison each morning in jolly spirits. Still, I managed
not to miss a day of work.

Until the hedge funds became a conspicuous problem, you
wouldn't have known from Jimmy's behavior or utterances
that anything was amiss. That might have been because in
terms of his immediate personal welfare nothing really was.

When our stock price peaked above $172 in mid-January 2007, Jimmy's 7 million shares were worth $1.2 billion. Two months later he announced the first-quarter results for fiscal 2007: we had made $554 million, an 8 percent increase over the previous year. A maddening correlation existed between our share price and Jimmy's demeanor. The higher it went, the more negative the effect upon his attitude and temperament. He became more aloof and full of himself. A Wall Street CEO has to make his presence known among his troops and within the community. It's a given that he must fly the flag on the charitable and business social circuits. Jimmy did very little of this. Maybe once in a while he would agree to be an honoree at a charity dinner, but he made no effort to conceal his impatience with these events. He preferred to be home in his pajamas playing bridge on his computer and actually bragged about that.

Such a mind-set couldn't help but impair certain business judgments. In May 2007, for instance, we had an arrangement with a bank in El Salvador that was selling out to Citigroup, an offer for half cash and half Citigroup stock, which the El Salvadorans intended to liquidate as quickly as possible. A native of El Salvador who worked for us in Boston went down there and came back with an agreement that allowed us, as soon as the buyout closed, to acquire the stock for 1 percent less than the most recent price, which was around $52. More than 14 million shares were involved. The closing was set for 10:00 a.m. on a Friday but a glitch arose and it couldn't close until 2:00 p.m. For no good reason, in the interim Jimmy decreed that we were backing out. Warren and I were in his office when he called Kenny Savio, our head of equity block trading, and told him we weren't doing the trade. When Kenny objected, Jimmy hung up on him. Warren and I looked at each other and I said, "Jimmy. That's not right. To hang up like that is ridiculous. We can make this work. We can renegotiate to take less of the stock if you like. But you can't just kill the whole deal and walk." His approach was pointlessly dictatorial, but finally we got him to bend. We ended up buying all 14 million shares, couldn't move the whole amount, and were long 2 million over the weekend. But Monday morning we came back and sold that and it turned out to be an excellent deal. That example typifies the way Jimmy conducted himself.

I accepted that Jimmy's personality was what it was and I rarely saw value in a direct confrontation. Instead, I offered occasional insights that I hoped would enhance his self-awareness. Why was it that a single elevator in the lobby had to be reserved for one person when we had thousands of employees coming and going all day long? In a gesture of noblesse oblige, I suppose, Jimmy modified that arrangement to an hour each morning, as if that solved any potential problem.

"Want to help your image around here, Jimmy?" I suggested that summer. "Get rid of the elevator thing. Everybody thinks it stinks."

"It's only from eight to nine in the morning," he said.

"Yeah," I said. "Just when everyone needs to use it."

We had a rule that you couldn't smoke in the building. I used to smoke an after-lunch cigar myself but quit when the city made it illegal. Jimmy kept right at it, in the lunchroom, in his office. It indicated an arrogance that manifested itself in ways minor and major. In early 2007, Warren had come to me to talk about Jimmy. He said, "He's irrational. We've got to do something," and I reminded him that I didn't believe in caucusing. I told him, "Warren, this conversation never happened."

Jimmy and Warren had a knotty history, like a rocky marriage in which neither party is willing to pay the price of a divorce. Warren's talents were obvious to all and it was generally assumed that when it came to the matter of succession, he had a slight edge over Alan Schwartz. But that did not curb Jimmy's periodic compulsion to put Warren in his place. For years, Warren had supported Democratic political candidates. Jimmy was a Republican who thought George W. Bush was doing a great job. In July 2004, Warren participated in a conference call with other business leaders who supported John Kerry's presidential candidacy, and it was subsequently reported that he had pointedly criticized President Bush. Instead of reacting immediately, Jimmy waited twelve days—in the meanwhile, Warren and his team advanced to the finals of the masters division of the national bridge championship, a tournament from which Jimmy's team had already been eliminated—and then sent an email to the entire firm harshly criticizing Warren for allegedly promoting his own political beliefs as if he were speaking for Bear Stearns institutionally. It was terribly embarrassing to Warren. It was embarrassing to everyone. Warren's friends called me and said, "How could Jimmy do that to Warren?" I didn't say anything. A year later, in 2005, Jimmy told me, "Warren has been absolutely perfect. He's been conducting himself beautifully, and I attribute that to that memo I sent." I looked at him as if he were crazy. The memo was unnecessary and degrading.

Not that Warren didn't make boneheaded moves of his own. Around the same time that Jimmy was congratulating himself for attempting to humiliate Warren, we bid on a very large block of stock to be sold by Nabors Industries, an oil-and-gas drilling and servicing company whose CEO was a good friend of Warren's. We were outbid and our competitor had a very successful transaction. In frustration, I guess,

Warren distributed a seriously impolitic memo criticizing the block-trading desk. Kenny Savio and I had been directly involved in the bidding strategy, and I thought it was wrong of Warren to broadcast this complaint—something you just *don't* do. Whenever you bid competitively you win some and you lose some. This gave me a little peek at an uncharming aspect of Warren's character.

But it couldn't hold a candle to Jimmy's megalomania, which was expressed most blatantly in his approach to the company stock. We had a rule that senior managing directors had to receive at least 50 percent of their compensation each year in the form of Bear Stearns stock. This was not a stock *option*, it was stock itself, at the prevailing market price. The IRS recognized this as deferred compensation that didn't vest for five years. At which point you were a fool not to sell it because the tax then became due. If you pay the tax and the stock later goes down, then what have you got?—a fundamental question that I'm not sure ever occurred to Jimmy. As far as I know, he never sold anything. The shares he held the day JPMorgan bought us consisted mainly of a career's worth of accumulated deferred compensation.

I then held 15,000 shares, plus about 200,000 that hadn't yet vested. I'd been consistently selling Bear Stearns stock for more than a decade. If I hadn't done so I would have been stuck with 8 million or 10 million shares at the end. We were the only major corporation I know of that didn't give its retiring CEO or chairman a huge benefits package. Our policy: no pension, no country club memberships or chauffeur or airplane privileges or life insurance or perks for spouses—none of that. When people left, they left. As I was largely responsible for the policy, I obviously knew that I had to plan for my own retirement, which I did by routinely diversifying my holdings, just as I always had, just as any experienced risk manager does. If you're an insider and you own a lot of stock, the securities laws limit your potential liquidity, and I never wanted to be in that position. I sold stock at a wide range of prices. If I got $80 a share, I assure you that when it later went to $150 I never second-guessed myself—because most of the securities I bought with my Bear Stearns proceeds performed just as well. On several occasions I advised Jimmy to diversify at least somewhat. I might as well have been talking to a fire hydrant. From Jimmy's warped point of view, selling my stock somehow delegitimized my opinions.

Once, when he objected to my questions during an executive committee meeting, he dismissively said, "What do you care? You don't own any stock."

"Your problem is you own too much," I told him.

By 2006, when I began to ask with increasing frequency "Why are we doing this?" (or that), it was an echo of my misgivings during the technology-stock boom in the 1990s. Why were we offering leveraged-buyout financing on the terms that some of our investment banking clients insisted upon? "The things they're asking us to do are crazy," I told Jimmy. "Expecting us to lend money and also guarantee the sale of the bonds they plan to issue to pay us back? Expecting us to put up the value of the equity until they feel like taking us out with an IPO?"

"This is one of our biggest sources of income," Jimmy replied. "Do you want us to cut that off? Do you want to quit doing business?"

That missed the point; I wanted to stay in business, but we needed to be more selective.

In midsummer 2007, I noticed that our distressed securities area owned an unhealthy overload of airline stocks, plus about a billion dollars of bonds issued by the airlines during debt reorganizations that were due to get converted to common stock. Delta and Northwest Airlines were selling above $20 (but six months later would be below $12). Jimmy didn't know we had this stuff. I said, "Why do we want to own airline stocks? For a hundred years no one has ever made money owning stock in anything that flies."

Jimmy said, "If we sell these now, they'll quit"—meaning the people running our distressed securities area.

What? When you run a big company, you can't be afraid of the people who work for you. I told him, "If you're the chairman and CEO and you see something that doesn't make sense, don't you have the right to tell that to your employees? Can't we talk about these positions?"

Jimmy: "I don't think so."

That exchange epitomized a disengagement on Jimmy's part that over time had become more pronounced and more baffling. During the last week of June, along with the executive committee's deliberations about whether to bail out the lenders to Ralph Cioffi's hedge funds, we confronted two other major agenda items. The most exasperating, from where I sat, was an absurd proposal to buy back 10 percent of our own stock, at a cost of roughly $1.5 billion, a ploy advocated by Jimmy and our chief financial officer, Sam Molinaro. Their rationale—placating shareholders by boosting our return on equity—ignored the gratuitous burden this would place upon our liquidity. No, no, there was nothing to worry about, Sam maintained, because we were "swimming in money"—in essence, the same response I'd gotten a couple of years earlier when I questioned the investment banking risks we were incurring. "Where are we getting the money to pay for these things?" I'd asked back then, and was assured that we could address any liquidity concerns by selling long-term bonds. Before becoming CFO, Sam had been a competent comptroller, but he'd never been a risk manager and I hadn't seen evidence that he should be the person telling me how much liquidity was enough.

I minced no words: "This is nuts. There is no such thing as having too much capital in this business." The discussion became so heated that Warren and Alan, as a compromise, suggested that we buy only a million shares, which were then selling for $139. Of course, I opposed that, too, which made it 4 to 1 (and the minutes reflect that). Before the vote, Jimmy, as gracious as ever, told me, "You don't have to vote. Everybody knows how you feel."

The buyback began the next day, a Tuesday, and was to continue for four more days—200,000 shares per day. Imagine my unhappy surprise, then, when I came in to work the following Tuesday and learned that the block trading desk was processing an order to buy another 200,000 shares. Without consulting anyone—except, perhaps, Sam—Jimmy had given instructions to acquire 600,000 shares more than the executive committee authorized. I immediately called his office and was told that he was in a meeting of the management and compensation committee, during which he apparently mentioned to Alan what he'd done. Alan promptly canceled the orders. (Though not before 60,000 shares had already been bought.)

That same day, the Blackstone Group announced its leveraged buyout of Hilton Hotels Corporation for $26 billion—what would prove to be, for the time being at least, the end of a succession of once unimaginably extravagant private-equity-driven LBOs. The previous Friday, the executive committee had held its final deliberations over whether or not to participate as a lender to Blackstone. If we did, our $10.7 billion commitment would make it one of the largest deals we'd ever been involved in. As with the stock buyback, my apprehension focused upon liquidity: what potential stress would this place upon our ability to fund our routine trading and clearing operations? On top of which we faced a potential public relations mess if, simultaneous with the hedge funds crisis, we backed out of the Hilton deal. Our mortgage-financing people thought that moving the Hilton bonds would not be easy but that it was a high-grade business and so, barring a catastrophe, we could sell them and do very well. In addition to the standing committee, I asked a dozen senior people from the fixed-income areas to attend. Those who couldn't be there in person participated by telephone, the largest gathering ever during an executive committee meeting. (The minutes reflect that, too: "The following members of TBSCI-EC [The Bear Stearns Companies, Inc., Executive Committee] were present (with Mr. Cayne absent) constituting a quorum: Alan C. Greenberg, Samuel L. Molinaro Jr. (via teleconference) Alan D. Schwartz (via teleconference), Warren J. Spector . . . Also in attendance were: Steven Begleiter, Simon Breedon, James Conopask, Joseph Geoghan, Lonny Henry, Jeffrey Mayer, Craig Overlander, Randy Reiff, Robert Steinberg, Lawrence Alletto, Keith Barnish, and David Glaser.") Their input mattered because I wanted the best and the brightest to tell us whether we were being dumb or smart. There was one notable absentee: Bear Stearns's chairman and chief executive.

The summer weekend routine that Jimmy allowed himself began Thursday afternoon, when he headed from the office to a nearby heliport and boarded a charter that seventeen minutes (and $1,700) later would deposit him in Deal, New Jersey, where he owned a home on the shore. At times, the helicopter would land at the Hollywood Golf Club, where he could regally stroll to the first tee for an afternoon round of golf. Typically he would play three more times that weekend and chopper back to the city Sunday evening.

Without having conducted a survey, I think I'm correct in saying that most senior managing directors at Bear Stearns had second homes and many liked to get away early when they could on summer weekends. Everyone understood the policy: whenever you were away from the office on a workday, a designated person had to know where and how to reach you as quickly as possible. If your participation was required at a meeting but you couldn't physically attend, that's why God created conference calls.

Everyone but Jimmy. The hour of the Hilton financing discussion, it seemed, didn't work for him. And that was why? *Because it conflicted with his golf date.*

I'm sorry to say that, in spite of my lifelong resolve to move forward continually, this particular example of Jimmy's egotism, tone deafness, and clueless contempt for the rest of us still provokes my outrage: for a $10.7 billion deal, he wouldn't even rearrange his tee-off time.

Almost without fail (one exception being when a serious medical matter kept him out of the office for a couple of weeks), if Jimmy was away for personal reasons and golf wasn't a factor, bridge was. In mid-July, he and Warren each spent more than a week in Nashville playing in a national tournament. For many hours a day, both were unreachable — never mind that the executive committee continued to meet at least once a day to grapple with the exigencies and likely consequences of the imminent bankruptcies of both hedge funds. Monday, July 30, when they returned to 383 Madison, was the date of the formal filing of the petitions to liquidate the funds. Two days after that, Jimmy called Warren into his office and insisted that he immediately resign as president. Two days after *that,* before the news about Warren became public, Standard & Poor's changed the rating on our senior corporate debt, downgrading it to "negative outlook." This news we regarded in the same spirit that we would have greeted a bulk mailing of anthrax spores.

The damage-control response was to arrange for a conference call that afternoon with more than two thousand analysts. The call's purpose, needless to say, was to offer reassurance: yes, we've taken some lumps in the mortgage-backed securities markets, but we've responded aggressively and confidently because our liquidity is strong, our capital base is rock-solid, and we maintain steadfast relationships with our traditional lenders. That message, however, was not at all what the analysts and the press took away. Jimmy spoke first, then Sam, followed by our treasurer and chief risk officer. When it came time for questions from the analysts, the first one pertained to our stock price. Ironically—or perhaps not—the questioner asked whether we had given thought to buying back our stock. He directed it to Jimmy, but after an interval of silence, Molinaro interjected that Jimmy had stepped out of the room.

When I subsequently heard about this, my reaction, which more and more had become a default response to Jimmy's acts of commission and omission, was incredulity: He *left* the meeting? Eventually two interpretations of this episode emerged: (1) Jimmy didn't consider the analysts' call worth sticking around for; (2) in actuality he hadn't left the room but couldn't answer the question because he was literally dumbstruck. I assumed the former—yeah, that sounded like Jimmy. After all, it was a Friday, the helicopter and golf course beckoned, and the clock said to head for the exit. In time, though, I inclined towards the equally plausible explanation that he had never even left his chair but was too traumatized to speak. (What finally led me to that conclusion was Jimmy's insistence to the contrary.) Either way, it added up to the fact that in a time of crisis he flatly wasn't up to the task.

Net effect: the damage-control initiative accomplished anything but. It surely didn't help when Sam, in an excess of candor, remarked that conditions in the fixed-income markets were as bad as anything he'd seen in more than twenty years. The instant the call ended, the equity and bond markets reacted. Our stock dove 8 points and took the Dow with it, down almost 300 for the day. Not what we needed.

The precipitous decision to fire Warren belonged in the same category. I didn't question Jimmy's prerogative, but the timing seemed wrong. Here was a piece of negative news whose release happened to be within our control. Alan Schwartz and I did everything we could to slow Jimmy down. Wait until after Labor Day, we advised. Let's at least have the benefit of an autopsy before doing anything drastic, we pleaded. But Jimmy didn't want to listen. "No," he said. "I'm doing it now."

Warren's departure exposed us to a whole new set of problems. Certainly there were legitimate grounds for Jimmy's unhappiness, but sound reasons existed not to fire him abruptly. No one in the firm could fathom the entire fixed-income side as well as Warren, and his insights and institutional memory could have provided a roadmap for our collateral and trading strategies as we attempted to liquidate not just the hedge funds but our own positions.

It wasn't as if I didn't have my own problems with Warren, in matters of both substance and style. As I've previously said, he and I exercised the only two votes on the risk committee. Those Monday meetings were attended mostly by traders, but managers from other departments were also present. I don't know who in the room besides Warren had a thorough grasp of the panoply of fixed-income derivatives we traded. My primary concern was seeing to it that, in the most basic sense, we truly were managing our risk, which meant having the proper hedges in place. The priority was to move our inventory, especially our low-grade bonds, which were mostly mortgage-backed. The guys in the mortgage department would report our long positions, which from late 2006 on kept going up. Provided that the shorts also kept going up, our downside was limited—right?

If we were long $60 billion in mortgages and had $40 billion in short positions, I assumed our exposure was $20 billion. But what if we were long apples and short oranges? Then we weren't necessarily hedged at all, were we? That, alas, to a painful extent proved to be the case. Multiple variables contributed to an extremely complex dynamic, yielding consequences that I hadn't previously encountered. What if we'd gone long on mortgages while shorting stuff that didn't have the same degree of risk, so when the longs went down, the shorts didn't. In other words, what if, notwithstanding our best intentions, our exit strategy didn't really provide an exit?

By June, as it proved harder to deleverage our mortgage-backed holdings without absorbing huge write-downs, Warren's people tried different sorts of hedges. It became downright frantic. They were covering the debt longs by shorting certain stocks, all the while foraging for new ways to hedge the longs. Those hedges worked for a while—until they didn't. With so many other institutions in an identical squeeze, new strategies had decidedly brief half-lives.

Given my reputation as a highly adept risk manager, I've been criticized for not having raised an alarm about the magnitude and overleveraging of our fixed-income holdings. At the same time, anyone closely familiar with Bear Stearns's decentralized business model and with Warren's imperious habits recognized the pitfalls of dealing with him. Knowing what I know now, I would have inquired more pointedly whether we were short the same things we were long. However, Warren insisted upon being 100 percent in control of his department. He'd been tremendously successful and he didn't want anyone encroaching on his turf. Interfering in his bailiwick would have been like *Mutiny on the Bounty*; I would have found myself in a rowboat. During risk committee meetings I never hesitated to interrogate the equity traders, as that was my area. When it came to fixed-income, though, it was only after Warren left the firm that I fully appreciated just how leveraged we were.

After the serial tribulations of the summer, a period of relative stability returned in the early fall. Things improved a little because the severity of our losses diminished. Nevertheless, partners and retired partners who had stock they could sell were quietly doing so. Who could blame them?

In early August, coincident with Warren's firing, the *Wall Street Journal* reported that we were seeking fresh capital and had been in discussions with China CITIC Group, the largest investment bank in China. A few weeks later, Jimmy flew to Beijing. For a good part of the fall I was preoccupied with my health and wasn't privy to many details of whatever major investment might have been in the works. Jimmy's China discussions would drag on for months, and in the end nothing would come of them.

Meanwhile, I seriously contemplated leaving Bear Stearns. For an accumulation of reasons, I wasn't happy, not least because Jimmy seemed less interested than ever in what I had to offer. If I said something was yellow, he said it was green — end of discussion. Finally, while Jimmy was away for several days in late November playing in another bridge tournament, I went to see Alan Schwartz and told him of my intention to quit. I'd taken enough crap from Jimmy and had no appetite for more. Alan urged me not to do it, and when Jimmy returned he did the same. (The account of the latter conversation as presented by Jimmy in *House of Cards* is beyond preposterous and unworthy of rebuttal.)

What finally persuaded me to stay was my recognition that the firm could ill afford the repercussions if I were to resign. Whatever the intramural realities of the atmosphere and decision-making process within Bear Stearns, more than anyone else — if for no other reason than sheer longevity — I personified the history and pedigree and historical standards of the firm. I didn't want to jeopardize any of that. I still believed that we were in business today so that we would be in business tomorrow.

As circumstances evolved, instead of me leaving, it was Jimmy who would soon be out the door.

11

THE RESULT OF THE NEGOTIATIONS BE-
tween Bear Stearns and China CITIC Group—actually, the
lack of a result—had no bearing upon our eventual destiny.
As a vivid rendering of Jimmy Cayne's truest colors, though,
it managed to say a lot. My familiarity with the specifics of
the negotiations is sketchy, also entirely secondhand. I was
not consulted at any point, nor do I recall Jimmy even dis-
closing that discussions with China CITIC were taking place.
Given that the whole thing dead-ended, this was just as well; I
was spared the usual exasperation along the way. And I hardly
needed to hear the fine details in order to get a firm fix on the
motivation for this folly.

Throughout the late summer and fall of 2007, we were
party to a succession of minor dalliances—expressions of interest from potential strategic investors who, in theory, might
have helped shore up our capital and liquidity. We were also
the object of at least as many baseless rumors along those
lines. Basically this was fallout from our hedge-fund bailout,
fed by conjecture that we were now vulnerable and that our
stock price had become cheap. Complicating all the speculation was uncertainty about how analysts and the market in
general might react if we were to disclose, say, a $5 billion
equity investment from Hedge Fund X or Bank Y. Would that

be seen as a solid vote of confidence? Or a sign that the immensity of our debt justified serious concerns about our liquidity? Strength or weakness? Another factor in the intrigue was our policy tradition of giving merger and buyout feelers the cold shoulder, a reflex rooted in the assumption that no other corporate culture could absorb or be absorbed and smoothly integrated with ours. Without a doubt, any injection of outside capital that compromised our independence would have major repercussions where our morale, identity, and collective sense of purpose were concerned.

The advance work that preceded Jimmy's Labor Day trip to China was overseen by Donald Tang, who had long guided our efforts to establish a stronger Bear Stearns presence in Asia. Donald was hired by Jimmy and he was a jewel, smart and very likable. Born in China, educated there and in California, he became president and CEO of Bear Stearns Asia while he was still in his thirties and later vice chairman of the entire firm. In spite of Donald's efforts, for many years we had lost money in China, thanks to a chronic failure to control costs. Even after we began to get a handle on the overhead, quantifying results remained problematic—a consequence of the diffuse types of business we pursued and the fact that not all of them lent themselves to conventional cost-benefit analyses. Symbols and formalities mattered a lot more in Asia than in the States and I'm sure Jimmy's vanity and ego always got a thorough workout when he went there. That certainly had been an issue in 1993, when he began trying to cultivate a franchise in China and urged me to relinquish the title of chief executive officer so that he would be accorded the appropriate respect.

The China CITIC discussions consumed months and represented an investment of thousands of man-hours and hundreds of thousands of dollars (a conservative estimate, I'm sure). On October 22, at Jimmy's insistence, a not-yet-really-a-deal deal with China CITIC was announced by Bear Stearns with a fanfare that left people inside and outside the company scratching their heads. As I've pointed out already, whenever Western capitalists think they have an agreement, that is, from the Chinese perspective, the moment to begin serious negotiations. At that point we needed fast action, not a long negotiation plus more negotiation. What Jimmy believed had been set in motion, in terms of real anticipated results and ramifications, is anybody's guess.

China CITIC, according to the deal terms, would make a billion-dollar equity investment in us and . . . we would make a billion-dollar convertible-debt investment in China CITIC. If the math on that has you stumped, let me help you out. The net dollars headed our way: zero. For many of us, Jimmy's characterization of this as "a groundbreaking alliance" had an unmistakable emperor's-new-clothes ring. Somehow we would be gaining access to certain of China CITIC's investment opportunities and in turn they would gain access to our asset-management clients. And what were Jimmy's criteria when he described this as "the best [deal] to cross [his] desk in forty years?" That one still has me stumped.

The impetus for all of this, unquestionably, was Jimmy's need to do something that seemed *big* and for which he could claim maximum credit. Genuine substance would perhaps materialize down the road. Meanwhile, appearances trumped all else. (Could China CITIC have been driven by the same imperative? Unlikely. Did they have a clue how disengaged Jimmy had allowed himself to become from the urgent problems that bedeviled Bear Stearns? Equally unlikely.) Whether others within the firm believed that China CITIC represented a solution to anything, I can't say. But the market barely blinked. To generate the excitement Jimmy hoped for would have taken something really big—i.e., a full-on merger—and thus far there were no indications that he was interested in a merger. I wasn't initiating or pushing one myself, nor did I possess that prerogative in the firm hierarchy, but I never stopped insisting that we needed to do everything possible to consolidate our capital and liquidity.

I've since wondered whether, at that juncture, Jimmy honestly felt in control or was his energy focused on maintaining a workable illusion of control. The most urgent of our problems lay in the fixed-income area, and our leveraged holdings there—the collateral for the borrowing that fueled our business on a daily basis—continued to lose value. The only person at Bear Stearns who had ever truly been able to get his arms around the totality of that situation, Warren Spector, no longer worked for Bear Stearns. His successors, Jeff Mayer and Tom Marano, were both highly regarded, first-class traders, but by the time they took over it was late in the game. Not that Jimmy would ever concede the point, but the firing of Warren complicated his ability to lead in ways from which he would never recover—an outcome, as it happened, that became a certainty when, one morning before Jimmy even left the house to go to work, he got mugged.

It came in the form of a humiliating story that appeared on the front page of the *Wall Street Journal* on November 1. Written by Kate Kelly, it depicted Jimmy as arrogant, negligent, and obtusely self-involved. It had never occurred to him, obviously, that he could be publicly confronted with glaring evidence that his bridge and golf games took precedence over his chief executive responsibilities. During July, according to the *Journal*, when the hedge-fund crisis was a seven-day-a-week preoccupation, he spent ten workdays in the office. Kelly dug up the cost of his weekend helicopter rides, ferreted out his tee-off times, and mocked him for bragging about his stash of $140 cigars. His aversion to business travel was such that if George W. Bush wanted to solicit Jimmy's economic advice, it seemed, he'd have to come to 383 Madison. When a visitor introduced Jimmy to her eleven-year-old son, he told her, "That kid's got a rotten handshake. He's going nowhere in life." During a dinner with analysts in the spring of 2007, he left the impression that he was unconcerned about the deteriorating market for mortgage-backed securities. Though the article gave Jimmy credit for the 600 percent rise in the price of Bear Stearns stock since he became CEO, that accomplishment was obliterated by one revelation that would endure as the most indelible image of his carelessness: "Attendees say Mr. Cayne has sometimes smoked marijuana at the end of the day during bridge tournaments. He also has used pot in more private settings, according to people who say they witnessed him doing so or participated with him." In response to a description of one such scene in the men's room of a hotel lobby in Memphis in 2004, Jimmy told the *Journal*, "There is no chance that it happened. Zero chance."

The same day the article appeared he sent an email to the entire firm. "I remain, as I have been for many years, intensely focused on our business," he vowed. As for the allegation of "inappropriate conduct outside the firm," he reiterated that this was "absolutely untrue." If it weren't for the embarrassment that now hung over the entire firm, compounded by the likelihood that many of our competitors were enjoying this situation, his kicker would have been laughable: "And don't be distracted by the noise. I certainly am not."

Like hell. If he failed to grasp how thoroughly he had tarnished his reputation, it was testimony to the amazing capacity for denial that the doomed often possess. I hadn't finished reading the *Journal* story myself when I knew that this was the end. He was dead, from self-inflicted wounds. He was an albatross. Sooner rather than later, the board would have to ask him to leave. Did I discuss it with anybody? No. Did I go running around the firm saying he had to go? No, because I don't do those things. But I knew that nobody believed his denials. Did I actually care whether or not he smoked pot? Here's what I cared about: Bear Stearns, its employees, and its shareholders. I knew that he'd been smoking pot for years. At bridge tournaments I'd seen it myself. Did I ever see him do it in the office? No. Had I heard that he did that? Yes.

As this freak show played out, we were getting no closer to solving our fixed-income problems. Despite all the experience, skill, and dedication of our personnel in that area, I didn't feel reassured that we had the wherewithal to do much about it. After Warren left, Jimmy designated Sam Molinaro as our chief operating officer, a hat he would wear while remaining chief financial officer. As soon as I got the announcement, I marched up to Jimmy's office and said, "How can you do this without discussing it with anybody? This is the most ridiculous thing I ever heard of. This guy can't possibly be qualified to be a chief operating officer. He's never bought a security, he's never sold a security, he's never had clients, and you know what I think of his judgment."

The decision to buy in a million of our own shares had proven to be, as I had predicted, a mistake. We had paid about $139 a share and that was the last time anyone saw that price. By mid-August, it was trading at $103. A couple of months later, it had an uptick and was over $120. Sam said to me something to the effect that people who'd been smart enough to buy it at $110 or $115 had "made a lot of money."

I asked him, "Sam, when you say people made a lot of money, do you know that any of them sold stock?"

No, actually, he didn't.

"Then I don't think you should go around saying that. Not only did they not make a lot of money, I don't think they made any."

In the fall, when the share price briefly got up to $128, I saw that Sam had put in an order to buy stock for some employees for the deferred compensation plan. He thought $128 was cheap and I thought otherwise. In that instance, I was at least able to get the order canceled.

As usual, though, when I recited to Jimmy the reasons why I thought Sam was the wrong candidate to be chief operating officer, I was wasting my breath.

"It's my decision," he said. "I did it and that's that."

By then, of course, I spoke with Jimmy only when I considered it absolutely necessary. We saw each other every Monday afternoon when the executive committee met, but our discussions were strictly business. Though I never wavered in my belief that his ouster was imperative and inevitable, I didn't dwell upon when the other shoe might drop. Long after the fact, I became aware that a large constituency of senior managing directors, including members of the management and compensation committee, so badly wanted Jimmy gone that they contemplated forcing the issue. Still, everyone accepted that this was a decision for the board of directors, not one that would be reached by popular referendum.

During a board meeting in mid-December, Jimmy himself broached the topic and proposed Alan Schwartz as his successor, a discussion that took place after Alan, Sam, and I had been asked to leave the room. I returned to my desk with no idea of what Jimmy was going to say. He was so proud, I never thought he would resign. He loved the title, loved the prestige and, owning as much stock as he did, I figured he'd have to be carried out. But I guess he'd read the newspapers. Later that afternoon, Alan, Sam, and I found out what had transpired. Because a timetable hadn't yet been established, though, this news wasn't for public consumption.

Nevertheless, the news began to leak out within a few days, just ahead of the announcement of our fourth-quarter results (our fiscal year ended in November). We had taken a $1.9 billion write-down of our mortgage-related assets, which gave us an $859 million quarterly loss, the first since we had gone public in 1985. Our net income for 2007 was $233 million, down from $2 billion in 2006. The executive committee had already decided that we would receive no bonuses for the year, a decision that required no deliberation because we all knew that we didn't deserve a penny. The previous month 650 employees, mostly in the fixed-income area, learned that they were losing their jobs—this in addition to two earlier rounds of layoffs that had eliminated almost a thousand positions. In the past, the firm had let people go when we closed certain departments, but a 10 percent reduction of our workforce was a whole other order of magnitude. Nothing like this had ever happened in the history of Bear Stearns.

At no point after that watershed board meeting did anyone that I knew of suggest that Jimmy's departure would be a mistake. Nobody begged him to stay on, there was no discussion that he or the board should reconsider. None. It was unanimous. Finally, on January 4, 2008, Alan went to see him and told him that the moment had arrived. Jimmy would retain the title of chairman of the board of directors but in a non-executive capacity. Formally, he was no longer CEO and no longer an employee of Bear Stearns.

Suffice to say, Jimmy has a memory of his valedictory that bears no resemblance to my own—a tearful series of gatherings ("there wasn't a dry eye") in which he was an object of universal affection. Figuratively, some people might have felt the urge to shed tears of joy, but my own recollection of that moment is of a prevailing sense of relief, not recrimination. Personally, I had nothing to say to the man. And what could he have possibly said to me? So we didn't exchange a single word.

12

WHOEVER COINED THE ADAGE ABOUT hindsight being twenty-twenty didn't make any allowance for astigmatism or myopia. Whose hindsight? And from what distance? A picture clarifies or blurs with the passage of time, and whatever image emanates at a given instant is colored by the biases of the observer. Knowing that my perceptions of the fall of Bear Stearns are inevitably somewhat subjective, I've tried to make sense of exactly what happened when and how this or that development along the way contributed to the ultimate outcome. I've wanted to get a fix on the moment when we ceased controlling our own destiny—not out of intramural curiosity but because that loss of control resonated and replicated globally. For those of us who across decades gave so much of ourselves to Bear Stearns, what took place during a single week in March 2008 was a watershed in our lives. With sufficient time and distance, as the context expanded, we could recognize it as the signal event of an enormous disruption that the world will be struggling to recover from for years to come.

While the wounds from our collapse were fresh and raw, Alan Schwartz was subjected to verbal assaults—including literally in-your-face tirades—from several Bear Stearns employees. Never having endured anything like that during my years as head of the firm, I can't say how I would have reacted to such provocation, but I thought Alan showed remarkable self-restraint and composure. He was as pained as anyone at Bear Stearns and he hardly deserved such abuse. Still, as CEO he unavoidably and understandably became the most obvious target. Shock, fear, grief, and anger were the dominant emotions, and some people, in panic and despair, just couldn't contain their outrage.

Alan was taken to task for failing to foresee the run on the bank that within four freakish days drained our liquidity, froze our credit, and forced us into a previously unthinkable Hobson's choice merger; for not extracting from JPMorgan a high enough price per share; for being a career investment banker instead of a trader; for not allowing Bear Stearns to declare bankruptcy (never mind that by any rational measure this was a suicidal nonoption). In some quarters, evidently, there's an unwritten rule that if your compensation exceeds a certain level you forfeit your right to be human and fallible. All the same, I can't think of any substantive reason why Alan should have to defend himself. I've come to the conclusion that by the time Jimmy Cayne left the building—literally, of course, not figuratively—the die was cast, the game was already over.

Although Alan tried as hard as he could to stabilize the ship, by January 2008 no individual could have intervened and reversed the damage already inflicted upon our balance sheet and our reputation. Our capital structure was withering, our inventory was stale, and it seemed as if whatever we held in our own account kept moving against us, confounding our hedging strategies on the fixed-income side. Our golden goose, as Haimchinkel and I years earlier had referred to our disciplined and dependable moneymaking juggernaut, was now merely a goose.

One morning not long after Alan took over, as he was becoming increasingly familiar with the dire specifics of our mortgage-backed bonds and derivatives, he called me and said, "You have no idea how bad this is. We're long all this crap." Despite that, I believe that he still must have had faith that we could somehow absorb our losses and regain our footing. The dismal results for the fourth quarter of 2007 — the whopping mortgage-related write-offs that had given us an $859 million loss — had hurt badly but there were indications that the first quarter of 2008, which ran from November through February, would show a return to profitability. That was the half-full perspective, at least.

From where I sat I didn't see how we were safely going to deleverage. How long would it take, and what would it cost, to unburden ourselves of our suffocating surplus of floundering mortgage-backed securities? For months, Joe Lewis, the British conglomerateur, had been acquiring our stock in huge blocks, until — go figure — he got up to 11 million shares, or 9.4 percent of the company. None of his maneuvers enhanced our capital because Lewis did his buying in the open market, not from us directly. During January and February, even with our stock trading in the $80 to $95 range, I didn't think we could be sold to another institution or investment group except at some knockdown price. This was not a thought I shared with anyone else, but I felt it.

I knew, without dwelling upon the possibility, that if the hedge funds and other institutions that were among our largest prime-brokerage customers ever decided, for any reason, that they no longer trusted us and began demanding their cash and securities, we would be helpless. I didn't *anticipate* that happening, but I fully understood that it could. Just as a cattle stampede can be caused by thunder, once that loss of confidence gained currency as a rumor, it would become a curse with a life of its own, and no matter what had triggered it, we absolutely would be finished.

I CAN'T say that when I showed up for work on Monday, March 10, the first day of the week that would be our last as a viable enterprise, I noticed anything unusual or sensed that the dikes were about to spring major leaks. Even when our stock began to drop that morning—by noon it was down more than 10 percent—I didn't feel alarmed. Over the previous sixty years I'd observed that stock prices fluctuate. Since the fall, the overall market had been drifting and financial stocks certainly were weakening, but nothing hinted at the implosion we were about to witness. Because our stock price had been trending southward for more than a year, this movement by itself didn't register as ominous. It took a couple of hours before I became aware of what had precipitated the slide: Moody's had downgraded to junk-bond status portions of fifteen different mortgage-backed debt issues that we had packaged and underwritten, including some so-called Alt-A bonds, a designation that was supposed to indicate solid quality and safety. By extension, the new Moody's ratings were bound to have a depressing effect upon other portions of our portfolio. The jolt to our share price reflected, in part, an assumption by some investors that our stock itself had been formally downgraded. Once such self-fulfilling pessimism (or cynicism) gathers momentum, a dike will spring more leaks than any available supply of pumps can withstand.

What happened next was unprecedented. I began hearing

from our traders rumors that some of our counterparties were expressing skepticism about our liquidity and were wary of dealing with us.

Had that indeed occurred? I was engaged in my usual routines—mainly, handling my clients' accounts—and was no longer immediately privy to urgent senior-level strategic deliberations or operational decisions.

I called Sam Molinaro and asked, "Is there anything going on that I should know about?" and he assured me that nothing was amiss with our liquidity. Kenny Savio, our head of institutional equities, had urged me to ask that question because customers were hounding him, wanting to know the same thing. When a reporter from CNBC called me, I told her forthrightly and succinctly: any concerns about our liquidity were "totally ridiculous."

Later I became aware that some of my colleagues objected at the time to my statement, complaining that I had spoken out of turn. What else was I supposed to do or say? A "no comment" or some other evasion, especially coming from me, would surely have deepened suspicions that something very dicey was bedeviling us—and nothing good would have resulted. I gave a truthful answer, as far as I knew, and I also knew that no other senior person in the company was available to field such questions. Jimmy, having rendered himself irrelevant though still officially chairman of the board was, fittingly, in Detroit that week, competing in the North American Bridge Championships. Alan was in Palm Beach, hosting Bear Stearns's annual media conference, a four-day gathering that brought together CEOs and other luminaries from throughout the media, telecommunications, and entertainment sectors for a state-of-the-industries summit. This had been months in the planning, it played to Alan's strengths as an investment banker who specialized in those areas, and he wasn't available to discuss breaking events in New York with CNBC or anyone else. Every financial editor in town knew my number. My habit of answering my own phone and responding to reporters' questions hadn't changed, but this by no means guaranteed that the caller would come away with anything useful. I handled the CNBC query in my customary blunt and unembellished manner.

Unfortunately, at some not precisely identifiable moment that day, we crossed into no-win territory. The 24/7 news cycle at CNBC, Bloomberg, and the other business-oriented cable networks was bound to grind away at this or any other fragmentary fact that might fit a narrative in which Bear Stearns or any firm of our stature appeared to be in trouble. Understand, please: in no respect do I blame the media for our travails. But considering the way the market works and "information" travels, whether the information is based upon verifiable fact or vague conjecture, once a tale of adversity has some wind at its back no one can spin that situation into a triumph.

Before the trading day closed, the Dutch bank Rabobank Group had told us that they weren't renewing a $500 million loan due to mature at the end of that week and probably wouldn't renew a $2 billion line of credit the following week. This turned out to be the prelude for an identical decision by another Dutch bank on Tuesday morning. Our borrowing costs and our collateral requirements would be going up — that is, *if* our largest lenders were willing to hang in there. Likewise, for some of our lenders as well as for particularly risk-happy speculators, a derivative cost of our borrowing —

namely, the spread on credit default swaps (CDSs)—had been gradually increasing for months and was now sharply accelerating.

The sum of our bank financing, short-term and long-term, was about $120 billion. Typically, a lender that wants to hedge its exposure can buy CDSs that offer protection in the event a borrower defaults. In one sense, it's an insurance policy for major banks and institutional lenders. A large volume of CDS trading, though, originates with lenders who risk substantial amounts because they like the odds that a default will reward them with *huge* amounts. The widening of CDS spreads—to oversimplify, the spread is the cost of the insurance premium, expressed as a percentage of the amount borrowed—indicated a growing belief that, sooner rather than later we very well might become insolvent. Concurrently, activity surged in the equity options market, with traders busily buying Bear Stearns puts, a form of short-selling. Our stock price on Monday was still in the mid-$60s but the option buyers were willing to pay for the right to force their counterparties to pay, say, $30 a share—meaning they had a hunch and a hope that the price would fall well below that. In essence, the puts were a wager that within nine trading days we would be in desperate straits or flat-out defunct.

Tuesday, trading in puts escalated, helped along by a steady stream of gloomy noise from CNBC and other outlets. Sam Molinaro reiterated to CNBC his denial that we were having liquidity problems. As the day progressed the situation was deteriorating, at least three hedge funds withdrew their cash, and one of those also pulled out all the securities from its prime brokerage account—tens of billions of dollars' worth. That afternoon, one of my clients, a family that had four accounts, asked us to wire all of their cash and securities to a major bank. They were scared, they told me, and when things calmed down they'd come back. Other than that, not another client of mine made such a request all week. If only the rest of the world had mustered similar faith and forbearance.

EVEN MORE unnerving than a long-term credit squeeze would have been an erosion of our short-term financing, and now that had begun. All major investment firms rely upon repurchase-agreement financing—or repos—to fund their daily activities. You pledge your own securities as collateral for billions borrowed overnight because you need the credit/ liquidity to lubricate and fuel your engine. At that point, our daily repo borrowing was running about $75 billion. Repo money gets repaid the following day and then the ritual re-peats, looping endlessly. Unless it stops.

Wednesday morning Alan Schwartz gave an interview to CNBC—he was still in Florida but due back in New York that afternoon—in which he made a game effort to address re-ports that we were having liquidity problems. Bear had an $18 billion cash reserve at the end of 2007 and that number hadn't changed. There was no crisis, he said.

I watched the interview from my desk, along with everyone else on the trading floor, and I thought Alan did as well as he could have. Not that it made a practical difference, however. More than a few people at Bear Stearns felt that he should have used the occasion to talk up our most recent quarterly earnings, which were due to be formally announced March 21. Throughout that week, there was an in-house clamor to re-lease the earnings report early. Logistical and regulatory ob-stacles related to marking the value of our fixed-income assets—or, if you're a stickler, our "assets"—made that a more complicated proposition than imagined. On CNBC, other than acknowledging that the numbers had improved, Alan didn't overenthuse. (The date of the earnings announcement eventually did get moved up three or four days but became moot when, in the interim, we went out of business.)

As Alan flew back to New York that afternoon, our repo lenders had begun falling away; at least $20 billion of overnight funding would no longer be at our disposal. Prime-brokerage clients had been withdrawing dollars and securities, siphoning away our cash reserves. We were also forced to divert more than $1.5 billion to satisfy repo lenders who had demanded more collateral. The mandate for that decision came directly from Alan, who was determined to avoid liquidating our collateral because the resulting fire sale would have discouraged untapped repo sources (as if any could be found). As the hedge funds retrieved their cash and the repo lenders sat on theirs, internal squabbles flared between the managers in prime brokerage and the repo desk. The prime brokerage guys had a point: we had become too reliant upon overnight borrowing. Traditionally repo had fought against greater long-term financing because it cost more. Now, in a liquidity crisis, we had the wrong balance and were about to find ourselves desperately short of our needs. Actually, the situation was about to make the transition from crisis mode to a full-blown race-for-the-exits bank run. And this was not the sort of bank run that would deliver us to a heartwarming *It's a Wonderful Life* conclusion. Something closer to *War of the Worlds* seemed more like it.

Thursday, the thirteenth, I showed up at the office at my usual time, left at my usual time, and in between did what I usually did—tried to make money for the firm. We began with roughly $18 billion of unrestricted cash and the feeble hope that it could carry us to the weekend. I handled my customer accounts, took calls, supervised equity trading with Kenny Savio, and kept on my game face. Retreating to my private office for a good cry wasn't in my playbook, so I passed on that. A casual observer probably wouldn't have gotten the impression that as the clock ticked we were hemorrhaging billions or that by sundown we would be functionally broke.

Throughout the day, Sam and our treasurer, Robert Upton, were occupied with determining how much financing would be available Friday, and it must have felt like fishing in a waterfall. The number was a moving target that traveled in only one direction. I kept apprised of events by communicating with Sam or Alan but still, at the end of the trading day, I headed out the door without having acknowledged to myself that we might not even open for business on Friday. Nor had I quite grasped that our fate now lay entirely in the hands of the federal government—that Timothy Geithner, the president of the New York branch of the Federal Reserve Bank, his boss, Ben Bernanke, and Henry Paulson, whom Geithner would succeed ten months later as Secretary of the Treasury, were calling the shots. By early evening, the most optimistic liquidity assessments showed that we had less than $5 billion in cash but, in light of the obligations that came due Friday morning, for all intents and purposes the figure was zero.

Kathy and I hosted a family dinner that night at the Park Avenue Café, on 63rd Street, to which we'd invited my granddaughter Melissa Frey's future in-laws and members of their extended family. I arrived at the restaurant ahead of the guests. Knowing that I'd have to excuse myself at some point during the evening, I wanted to find a quiet spot where I'd be able to have a phone conversation. At that hour, in a Greek restaurant about a mile away, Jamie Dimon, the chief executive of JPMorgan Chase, was also attending a family dinner. The first call I received came from Sam Molinaro, telling me that, at the behest of Geithner, Alan had interrupted Dimon's meal with a question that was a definite first for both: Bear Stearns needed a $30 billion lifeline to remain in business the next day. Could Morgan provide it?

Dimon's initial response was no, they could not. In ensuing conversations with Geithner, Bernanke, and Paulson, however, he quickly realized (as Alan had already figured out) that Bear Stearns's only alternative, a bankruptcy filing, carried a very real risk of global financial catastrophe, a looming calamity with incalculable consequences. Within an hour, a posse of Morgan bankers started showing up at 383 Madison, which they had no trouble finding because, conveniently (or eerily), it was directly across the street from their own headquarters. I assume that some of them must have shared elevators with the bankruptcy attorneys who were also filing in.

Our family dinner marked a happy occasion, but I would not describe it as leisurely. I missed a good part of the meal because I was participating with other Bear Stearns corporate directors in an emergency board meeting with a single agenda item: whether or not to authorize a bankruptcy filing. We agreed to do so but only in the event that no other financing had materialized before the Friday opening bell. After adjourning for a couple of hours—a window during which no angels descended from the firmament to fix the problem—we resumed at 10:30 p.m. in the partners' dining room at 383 Madison. This time I was physically present. Ambience-wise, the proceeding was less cheerful than most of the funerals I've attended. Alan and Sam did most of the talking. Jimmy, participating by phone from Detroit, had very little to say. (Only after I told him on Saturday that he ought to come back

to New York and Alan told him, point-blank, that he *had* to—
that there would be another PR fiasco if it became known
that, as Bear Stearns lay in extremis, Jimmy yet again was playing bridge—did he agree to leave.) At one point, a question
arose that Jimmy was the best qualified person to answer but,
give the man points for consistency, he had returned to the
bridge table and had to be summoned by his wife.

As the meeting broke up, I understood that we were still
trying to persuade JPMorgan to extend a $25 billion short-
term loan, but I fully expected that we would be filing for
bankruptcy the next day. At least I would be able to go home
and get some sleep, a luxury unavailable to Alan, Sam, and
many other senior Bear Stearns people, not to mention the
bankers and bankruptcy crews who had settled in for an all-
night ordeal.

About an hour before dawn, Geithner, Bernanke, and
Paulson had a conference call during which they elected
to perform what amounted to preventive cardiopulmonary
resuscitation—not the last time it would be administered
over the next seventy-two hours. With JPMorgan acting, in
effect, as a beard, the Fed would open its discount window—
the emergency credit source available to commercial banks
but not to investment banks—to avert our immediate demise.
Technically, Morgan would lend us $25 billion for what was
characterized as "up to twenty-eight days," but the true underlying risk would be borne by taxpayers. Already, every prerogative that pertained to our present and future had passed
out of our control, but this made it official.

The upshot was that we would live for at least one more
day. CNBC and the rest of the yakkers could refer to this
however they pleased—bailout, government rescue, what-

ever. What it meant was: we weren't dead yet. And the market seemed to concur—our stock jumped 10 percent, to $64—but wasted very little time before changing its mind. Within forty minutes of the opening, the price was $30. For the rest of the trading session, I felt as if I were watching an animal in its death throes. That afternoon, one of the leading financial industry security analysts downgraded our stock. Standard & Poor's, Moody's, and a third rating agency rendered comparable judgments about our long-term creditworthiness. Regardless of the intent and merits of the Morgan-Fed $25 billion credit facility, the public refused to go along. That sort of herd mentality makes you want to strangle the public, but I'm not so sure it was wrong.

I left for the weekend believing that bankruptcy was now an inescapable outcome. Morgan gave no indication of a genuine interest in acquiring us, and I didn't blame them. Days earlier, even as the repo lenders were slamming their doors, Alan Schwartz and many other people had mulled over worst-case scenarios in which we would be bought for $40 or $50 a share, a killer discount from our book value of $80.

Right. And who would buy us? Who *could* buy us?

By the time I reached the office on Saturday for an 11:00 a.m. directors' meeting, cold reality had plummeted several degrees. During Alan's ride home to Connecticut the night before, he'd gotten a call from Geithner and Paulson, telling him that they wanted to clarify a detail. (To this day, how such a detail had not been previously clarified remains a mystery.) "Up to twenty-eight days," they pointed out, did not mean the same thing as "twenty-eight days." As far as they were concerned, we had exactly two days to find a buyer or else face liquidation. Come Monday, the $25 billion loan would be off the table. That gave us until Sunday evening at 7:00 p.m. eastern time, when the Asian markets would open.

As Dr. Johnson (a distant cousin of Haimchinkel) observed, the prospect of being hanged tends to concentrate the mind.

Teams from Morgan had been back at 383 Madison since early Saturday morning, performing due diligence, trying to develop a coherent enough picture of our asset quality, liabilities, and liquidity predicament to make a formal bid. One other potential buyer, J. C. Flowers & Company, was on the premises going through the same exercise. J. C. Flowers was a former Goldman Sachs partner who had set up his own private equity shop in the late nineties. Despite his sterling reputation, his firm had nowhere near enough cash to buy us and too little time to round up additional funding. I never believed anyone other than Morgan had the resources and the personnel to do a deal.

The directors' meeting took place in a private dining room on the seventh floor. Most of the board members were still digesting the roller-coaster dramatics of the day before—and now this. Alan was as stunned by Geithner and Paulson's edict as the rest of us. The board's questions ran towards whether or not we had any negotiating leverage, was there any way to buy time, were there any other options? (No, no, and no.) Our advisors included H. Rodgin Cohen, of Sullivan & Cromwell, the foremost banking attorney in the country, and Gary Parr, the deputy chairman of Lazard, who had been working doggedly to try to come up with other prospective bidders. In the absence of an encouraging prognosis, the most positive thing about the discussion was that it didn't last long. When the meeting ended, around noon, we left knowing that we would soon return.

We heard nothing significant until we reconvened again around 7:00 p.m., and though what we then learned made no one happy, it at least gave us a definition of what we were now "worth." Morgan was willing to pay somewhere between $8 and $12 per share. Their due-diligence crews and lawyers still had a full night of digging and drafting in store, so a formal offer wouldn't be ready until Sunday morning.

As I've mentioned earlier, I arrived at 383 Madison on Sunday anticipating a board vote on that offer, only to be told that I might as well turn around. Again, it seemed, we were doomed. There would be no Morgan bid. A couple of hours earlier, Jamie Dimon had informed Geithner that they were dropping out, scared off by our mortgage-backed assets. Overnight they'd concluded that the toxic portion of our portfolio might exceed $200 billion; it just wasn't worth the risk.

Geithner, Paulson, and Bernanke, on the other hand, were thoroughly convinced that allowing us to file for bankruptcy represented a far more immense risk. So yet again we received CPR, this time in the form of a $30 billion nonrecourse government loan to Morgan. It had been approved by a vote of the Federal Reserve Board and would be collateralized by an equivalent package of our cherry-picked mortgage-backed securities.

Once word of this development reached 383, we were summoned back to the seventh-floor dining room, where we spent the next few hours ... waiting.

Given the size and nature of the Fed's commitment to Morgan, there wasn't a prayer that the bank's bid would remain where it had been twenty hours earlier. In buying us, Morgan obviously hoped to reap an enormous long-term benefit, but the circumstances had ushered all of us into the realm of moral hazard, where indulgence is prohibited and punitive discipline must be imposed. The moral hazard theory assumes that a party (say, the managers of a bank) that's insulated from the consequences of risk will be more inclined to behave imprudently or recklessly. That Bear Stearns had been designated the new archetype for moral hazard was revealed at 4:00 p.m., when Gary Parr reported that Morgan's price would be $4.

During the board's discussions the previous night, after we had been told to expect a bid between $8 and $12, the notion was floated—referred to as "the nuclear card"—that we should call the government's bluff. The price was too low, we were having none of it, let's file for bankruptcy, and see how everybody likes that. It goes without saying, I suppose, that this desperate strategy's leading enthusiast was Jimmy. Still, even he realized that this action categorically could not be allowed to happen. Now, however, he was back at it, profanely insisting that we were better off liquidating, we weren't going to stand for this, under no circumstances, they can take their lousy four dollars and . . .

It wasn't that no one else shared Jimmy's extreme frustration, but you don't have to be a brilliant card player to recognize an unplayable hand. As it was, the discussion of the demerits of $4 a share was promptly interrupted by another phone call to Parr from Morgan. In Paulson's estimation, a $4 price tag still represented moral hazard. "That sounds high to me," he was later quoted as having told Dimon. Whereupon the bid was cut to $2. Rog Cohen wanted to know whether this was negotiable, and Parr explained that the number had come from the government, not Morgan. In other words: no.

We all experienced momentary disbelief, followed by Jimmy wailing about not being wiling to take $2.

Two dollars is better than zero, I then said. Fifty cents is

183

better than zero. At least we're still alive and when you're alive good things can still happen. If you're dead—nada.

At 6:30 we voted, and it was unanimous.

In the week that followed, JPMorgan increasingly confronted deep-seated resistance to the $2 offer. Some of our largest shareholders—institutions, Joe Lewis—were not coy. They were willing to explore any machinations that might prevent the merger from going through. The market got the message, the arbs milked the skepticism, and by Tuesday our stock was trading at $8. For a change, our shareholders had gained a bit of leverage, thanks to a drafting peculiarity in the merger agreement. According to the deal terms, Morgan had committed for one year to finance our operations and absorb up to $30 billion of losses on the sale of assets. They had no recourse, however, if shareholders failed to approve the merger. Our employees owned 40 percent of the outstanding stock. In theory, Morgan could bring the matter to a vote as often as they liked, but if the majority held out, in twelve months we would be free to fend for ourselves or find another buyer.

Plainly, if Morgan wanted the deal to go through, they were going to have to raise the price. The result was an agreement that included an issue of new stock, along with a pledge that our board members would vote 5 percent of the outstanding shares in favor. Those concessions, along with shares that Morgan had been buying that week in the open market, finally guaranteed that when it came to a vote they would have a majority. The merger would be a stock-for-stock transaction that valued Bear Stearns at $10 a share. To mitigate the increased cost of the merger to Morgan, the Fed agreed to absorb any losses above $1 billion that the bank incurred in unwinding our mortgage-backed assets.

One shareholder who didn't wait around for the merger to be consummated was Jimmy, who sold his shares at $10.83, yielding $61.3 million. This outcome entitled him to membership in a rather exclusive club—consisting of individuals who have personally managed to lose more than $1 billion, not on paper but right in the wallet. What he wasn't entitled to, however, was the deep discount on commissions available to Bear Stearns employees. Someone from the order desk came to me and asked, "What do we charge him?" Jimmy was no longer an employee, he didn't earn a salary, so I told them to charge the standard commission for members of the board, a nickel a share or whatever it was. The trade cost $77,000, rather than the $2,500 maximum commission for employees. As always, I did what I felt was in the best interests of the firm. Nothing personal.

The approval vote on the merger took place May 29, in our second-floor auditorium. Approximately five hundred people attended. Alan spoke graciously. When Jimmy, still the non–executive chairman, took his turn, he said he was sad, said he was sorry, said "Words can't describe how bad I feel."

I sat in the front row. I'd already agreed to accept a position at JPMorgan Chase as vice chairman emeritus (as had Johnny Rosenwald), where I remain to this day. The meeting lasted less than ten minutes. When it was over I went upstairs and back to work.

EPILOGUE

As metaphors go, the image of a "meltdown" pained me. Did our man-made disaster really belong in the same league with the Chernobyl horror of 1986? None of the phrases that gained currency in the immediate aftermath of our failure suggested that the alarm, bewilderment, and dread would dissipate anytime soon—not "toxic waste" (the lowest rated and potentially least liquid class of securitized subprime mortgage debt), not "sausage factories" (the cynic's definition of investment banks that packaged and sold bundles of pooled mortgage-backed securities), and least of all "meltdown." It sounded hopeless and apocalyptic.

Commentators suggested that in the wake of our sudden collapse, panic was gripping the markets. Panic is not a feeling I've ever experienced personally, but I recognize it when I see or hear it. As tens of billions of dollars of asset "values" were disappearing, meltdown became the analogy of choice to describe the unquantifiable consequences of the global financial crisis. Like the power loss and surge that triggered the disaster at Chernobyl, the securities markets plunged by the fall of 2008, desperately rebounded, then plunged further—an irrational volatility that resembled hysteria.

During the weeks between our takeover by JPMorgan and the shareholder vote that finalized the purchase, the anguish within the Bear Stearns family wasn't much reflected in the behavior of the markets. In midsummer, the Federal National Mortgage Association ("Fannie Mae") and the

Federal Home Loan Mortgage Corporation ("Freddie Mac") began to falter under the stress of defaults by millions of sub-prime borrowers. These two institutions were the dominant secondary-market purchasers of American home mortgages and both were placed in federal conservatorship—in effect, nationalized—with the U.S. Treasury guaranteeing $200 billion of their commitments in exchange for almost 80 percent of their combined equity. Their futures were uncertain, their shareholders had gotten clobbered, and the necessity for a government rescue did not bolster confidence in banks whose assets were backed by Fannie and Freddie.

It took another few weeks of awful news, mainly from the residential and commercial real estate sector, to do away with the wishful illusion that the worst had already occurred. By September, the erosion of collateral values and the reckless overleveraging of that collateral had rearranged the fundamentals of the stock and derivative markets. Prices of virtually all publicly traded banking and finance-related securities no longer indicated real earnings or asset values but were instead driven by speculation about where and how the federal government might intervene next. The changes that took place during that extraordinarily intense month—the most profoundly momentous since 1929, in my opinion—permanently altered Wall Street's landscape, starting with its supposedly most invulnerable institutions.

Within a two-week span: Lehman Brothers teetered on the brink of insolvency and was almost taken over by Barclays and Bank of America before finally filing for bankruptcy; Bank of America agreed instead to buy Merrill Lynch, which meant that within a matter of hours two of the four remaining traditional investment banking firms ceased to exist; the other two, Goldman Sachs and Morgan Stanley, converted into bank

holding companies and thus technically ceased being investment banks themselves; American International Group (AIG),
the insurance colossus, was rescued by the U.S. government,
which received 80 percent of the company's equity in return
for a desperately needed $85 billion credit facility (later in-
creased to $160 billion); Warren Buffett invested $5 billion in Goldman Sachs and received preferred stock with a
10 percent coupon plus warrants that entitled him to buy a
big chunk of common stock and potentially earn billions if
Goldman's fortunes improved—a cash infusion that averted
the once inconceivable possibility that Goldman, which had
been one of AIG's major counterparties, would suffer the sort
of uncontrollable run on its capital and liquidity that had
done in Bear Stearns; Morgan Stanley sold 21 percent of its
equity to Mitsubishi, Japan's largest bank, in order to avoid an
identical fate.

The following month, President George Bush signed the
Emergency Economic Stabilization Act, which created the
Troubled Asset Relief Program (TARP) and allowed the government to purchase from banks up to $700 billion in bad
assets—the notorious toxic waste, mostly. The funds represented a collaborative effort by the U.S. Treasury, the Federal
Reserve, and the Federal Deposit Insurance Corporation to
halt a self-perpetuating credit crisis that was infecting economies around the world. The FDIC raised its deposit insurance
cap from $100,000 to $250,000 per account; the impetus was
identical to the motive in 1933, when the FDIC was established to quell the fears that had touched off bank runs by
panicked depositors. On October 14, two weeks after TARP
was created, the government revealed that it was deploying
$250 billion to purchase preferred equity in qualifying banks,
which could receive the money on a first-come, first-served

basis. In varying amounts, half of this amount went to the country's eight largest banks, including JPMorgan Chase, Bank of America, Wells Fargo, Citigroup, Morgan Stanley, Goldman Sachs, Bank of New York Mellon, and State Street. The program appeared to be putting most of those banks on the path to recovery. Less than a month later, though, TARP changed its own rules. Henry Paulson, the secretary of the Treasury, announced that instead of allocating TARP's remaining $410 billion to buy toxic assets, the money would be used for further recapitalization of U.S. banks. The reversal shocked the market—which had already demonstrated its capacity to be easily shocked—and also Congress, which had signed off on TARP in the first place because of its promise to remove toxic assets from the banks' balance sheets. If the federal government was now directly buying bank stocks, some investors feared that a contagion of widespread bank nationalizations, as with Fannie Mae and Freddie Mac, lurked just around the corner. The TARP game plan changed again during the dwindling days of the Bush presidency, when $13.4 billion was diverted to help General Motors and Chrysler. Under President Obama, TARP's stated objectives would continue to evolve—$350 billion was used to purchase spoiled assets, as originally intended, and $50 billion was allocated for direct assistance to homeowners trying to avoid foreclosure.

Much of the intensity during the final weeks of the 2008 presidential campaign had been attributable to the erratic behavior of the markets and a free-floating anxiety about the precariousness of the economy. Everyone—economists, politicians, the media, Joe the Plumber—had plenty to say, worthwhile and otherwise, about the pain and fears of those workers who had already been laid off or soon would be. Not that I recall hearing much sympathy for those who had lost jobs in the banking and finance industry. The rhetoric from both parties made the election choice seem to be as much about Wall Street versus Main Street as it was McCain versus Obama.

In light of all this rescue-focused frenzy in the fall of 2008, it's easy to forget that six months earlier—we are really talking ancient history—within hours of the announcement of our sale to JPMorgan, the Federal Reserve had declared that from then on it would open its "discount window" to investment banks, access previously reserved exclusively for commercial banks. Investment banks that presented high-grade securities as collateral would be able to borrow directly from the central bank. Bear's failure and the apprehension that it provoked—how panicked might the panic become, and with what consequences? what would a global bank run look like?—had forced this policy shift. All of this amounted to a rewriting of the rules regarding moral hazard. As applied to the banking and credit crisis, any institution treated by the government as if it were "too big to fail" by definition enjoyed an inherently unfair advantage over any banks not regarded as such. As the opposing fates of Lehman Brothers and AIG illustrated, the definition of too big to fail was quite flexible. In addition to the deterioration of its assets and capital, Lehman had been undone by its clients' lack of confidence. The failure of Fannie and Freddie only made Lehman look worse. Too big to fail was hardly a novel concept. Under the extreme stress of the credit crisis, they had become populist fighting words.

BEAR STEARNS can now be understood as the first major casualty, among so many more, of the credit crisis. As such, we became the poster child of the public's fascination with an

191

immense loss of wealth—which in turn added to the emotional and psychological burdens of our former employees. Our image as unapologetically aggressive, nobody's-fool traders had constituted the nucleus of our institutional pride. As for the widely held theory that our habits and methods had been so off-putting that our competitors welcomed our demise—I didn't buy it. Specifically, as I've already made clear, I reject the conspiratorial view that we were singled out for retribution because of our stance during the Long-Term Capital Management crisis. Still, I'm aware that many of our aggrieved employees felt differently and were outraged by the thought of such vindictiveness. I understood the impulse to search for a scapegoat. There was no shortage of candidates, starting—and for many people, stopping—with Jimmy. Warren Spector also got some votes. But the deeper the unease about the government's policy choices, along with the fact that the Treasury Department and the Fed were making up and frequently rethinking new rules as they went along, the more the cast of potential whipping boys expanded. It reflected a gut-level need to find a villain worthy of the despair that so many of our employees experienced. Less than half of our personnel were offered jobs by JPMorgan Chase, and even the fortunate ones who survived had lost an attachment to an institution with a singular culture and identity. They lost, as well, faith in the notion that the markets worked fairly and efficiently and that by doing what we had historically done best, our survival was a foregone conclusion. But there was no virtue in being a victim, just as there was no way to reduce to a simple explanation the events that resulted in our failure.

In an interview with *60 Minutes* in early 2009, Ben Bernanke stopped short of calling the decision to allow Lehman Brothers to fail a mistake, but he expressed misgivings about the handling of that particular crisis. Others, including the author James Stewart, have referred to the decision to allow Lehman to fail as "disastrous." I'm not sure why. The Fed, the Treasury, and the FDIC did everything they could to find a buyer for Lehman, as its CEO, Richard S. Fuld Jr. had been repeatedly advised to do for months, and in the end no potential buyer felt that the risk was worthwhile. Ironically, not until a post-mortem analysis was completed during the winter of 2010 did the absolutely outrageous fact emerge that throughout 2007 and 2008 Lehman had been cooking its books with accounting chicanery that temporarily removed illiquid assets from its balance sheet at the end of each quarter.

I can only assume that the driving logic behind the willingness to let Lehman fail was a resolve to avoid creating another Bear Stearns scenario. A month after our sale to JPMorgan, Bernanke told the Senate Banking Committee that the merger had been in the interests of Main Street: to increase confidence in the markets and preserve the current financial system. Having a direct involvement in that transaction, I can personally attest to the fact that the deal the government struck with Morgan was granted in good faith. At that time, there was no consensus that another bank might land in such dire straits as ours.

Fuld, frankly, had engineered a tremendous and, it emerged, fatally overleveraged expansion of Lehman's assets, including direct real estate investments, unlike any other traditional investment bank. The firm had also participated in corporate financings that left it holding positions it couldn't sell, thus undermining its liquidity. Bear turned out to have been fatally overleveraged, but our only significant direct real estate investment was 383 Madison. Everything we held ap-

peared on the surface to be highly liquid. That a lethal portion turned out not to be can be attributed to many factors,
including the fact that a misleading triple-A rating could fool
even those of us who believe we understood our risk exposure.

The Fed and Treasury did not save Bear Stearns. Rather,
the Fed allowed JPMorgan Chase to borrow against $30 bil-
lion of securities we owned. And JPMorgan was liable for the
first $1 billion in losses. By the time the Fed window opened
to investment banks, we were no more. A few months later,
investment banking was no more. The classic model of the
investment bank—Bear Stearns, Goldman Sachs, Lehman
Brothers, Morgan Stanley, Merrill Lynch, and our legions of
long-departed competitors—became unviable because no
such institution could withstand the sort of run that put us
and Lehman under and came very close to killing Goldman
Sachs. What used to be known as investment banks cannot
survive as stand-alone institutions—only if they're formally a
part of the banking system and are backed up by the Federal
Reserve and the FDIC. There will still be firms doing commission business, there will be boutiques that do merger-and-
acquisition and advisory work, but never an institution that
does the full line of investment banking services unfettered
by the sort of regulatory oversight that exists within the regular banking system. That's gone; it's a failed plan.

When I came to Wall Street there were hundreds of
so-called investment banks. Sixty years later five were left,
Bear Stearns included, so we must have done some things
right. It's true that we disappeared, but I can assure you that
the other four changed form also. The original species is now
extinct. I'm not sure how anyone is to appraise his or her career, but I know that my evaluation of my own isn't measured

in terms of "good" and "bad" deals, as if profitability were the sole criterion for success or failure. When JPMorgan took over Bear Stearns, I knew that the material, social, and private particulars of my life would not be transformed, for better or worse. Frankly, my primary concern was focused on the 14,000 people who worked for Bear Stearns and what would happen to them. We had a culture, we had long-term relationships, we had associates willing to give almost everything for the success of our enterprise. I was particularly moved by some of the developmentally challenged people who worked for us as messengers. To a person, these remarkable employees almost never missed a day of work. If there was a snowstorm they showed up. Subway strike? — they managed to get to work. I assumed, correctly, that JPMorgan could not hire all of them. I was able to identify every one of these employees (twenty-seven in all) and notified them that I would send each of them $200 a month, for the next six years, to show my appreciation for their service. In case they couldn't get a job, I wanted them to know that they would have something to live on in addition to their Social Security disability benefits. The first batch went out in May 2008. When the recipients open those checks, they're not thinking about who signed them, I trust, but about what they had given, year in and year out to all of us, and I hope they are remembering what Bear Stearns, at its best, represented.

During my six decades on Wall Street I had my share of good luck. I also had some bad luck, but only enough to make me really appreciate the good luck. I met some marvelous people who became lifelong friends and, in short, quite frankly, it was a great run.

My two siblings, with whom I remain extremely close, and I were raised in an almost idyllic home. I was very fortunate to meet Kathy and marry her twenty-two years ago. She has made my life. I have two children, Lynne and Ted, of whom I'm enormously proud; while I'm at it, I want to formally thank them for sparing me during their adolescence and young adulthoods so many of the problems I read about today. My grandchildren are a special bonus.

MY FATHER'S basic decency and common sense stand out as the most treasured gifts I received from my parents. When I was young I lapped it up and as I got older I learned never to underestimate the value or lose sight of Dad's simplest and wisest truisms.

Such as? I will give you a few:

If you own something you think is bad, sell it today because tomorrow it will be worse.

If a person with limited money wants to buy your product on credit, sell him a small amount. He can only beat you once. And if he becomes a success he will never forget you.

My father opened many stores and they consistently proved to be successful. But he told me that the day would come when he would open a store that seemed to have everything going for it and yet it would underperform. A few years later, he found a location in Norman, Oklahoma, home of the University of Oklahoma, and he was sure it would be a huge winner. It was anything but. Dad's prophecy had come true. It took years for that branch of Street's to become even modestly profitable, and he never knew why it was such a dog.

My father believed that unless you have a valuable patent, the real assets of any business are the people. The boss had to set an example that his associates would want to emulate and build upon. Dad never had a problem training and keeping good executives. He liked and respected them, they knew it and reciprocated, and it all worked.

If any of Dad's vendors was having a problem, he always gave them an order. If the vendor worked out of his lean years, he never forgot what my father did. And if he ever had a hot item, my father got special treatment. Dad had planted a seed and it paid off.

It was sixty-one years ago that I left Oklahoma City. But it seems like yesterday that my father called me aside at the train station and said, "I'll give you three pieces of advice: never make fun of a millionaire, never hit a cripple, and never have sex with an idiot." To the best of my knowledge, I've remembered all three.

ACKNOWLEDGMENTS

IF BEAR STEARNS WERE STILL A GOING concern, I suppose I would have written a book with a title more along the lines of *The Rise and Continued Rise of Bear Stearns*. There would have been less drama. Still, the underlying convictions and sentiments would have been identical.

Even in the competitive atmosphere that flourished at Bear Stearns, one of the hallmarks of the culture was the mutual loyalty of our employees to one another and to the overall enterprise. I recognized and enjoyed the benefits of this ethos from my earliest days at the firm, when John Slade gave me my first break and Harold C. Mayer, one of the founding partners, befriended me. Despite my complicated relationship with Cy Lewis, our reciprocal loyalty was never in doubt; Cy was full of tremendous energy and drive, and once he sized me up, he encouraged and trusted me to do what I could do best.

I remain equally grateful to a number of other colleagues. John Rosenwald has been a partner of mine for fifty-six years, and we are as close now as we ever were. I feel a profound appreciation for Johnny. Mickey Tarnopol, a true warrior and a huge producer of business, was a great friend who died much too early. There are so many others who contributed so much to our success, I wish I could list all of them.

I've long been aware that many colleagues have criticized me for an alleged lack of patience. Frankly, I think they're mistaken. In fact, I have tremendous amounts of patience—I just haven't ever used any of it. The most immediate witnesses to this phenomenon have been my assistants of many years, Laura Schreiner, Lisa D'Amore Mezzatesta, and Deborah Colaizzo. They have put up with what we can euphemistically describe as my multiple idiosyncrasies, functioning as my collective right hand (actually, *hands*) with a stalwart combination of dedication, unflappability, and humor.

My gratitude to Mort Janklow (the correct agent is as much a necessity as the correct money manager) and to Bob Bender, of Simon & Schuster.

My collaborator and fellow Okie, Mark Singer, managed at moments not to be a total pain in the neck. He's also a good speller. Thanks, Mark (especially for writing this paragraph).

To my family, no verbal expression of thanks captures my deepest feelings. First and foremost, my loving and supportive wife, Kathy, who has always set aside time from her own career to lend her guidance and insight in writing this book and in every day of our lives together. (She was the founder of New York Legal Assistance Group over twenty years ago and she has been chair of Cardozo Law School board of overseers for six years.) Kathy is truly beautiful, not only on the outside but on the inside as well. My daughter, Lynne, and my son, Teddy, always have been behind me in every aspect of my life, and my grandchildren have given me nothing but pleasure. My sister, DiAnne, and my brother, Maynard, were always cheering me on, and many other members of my extended family did nothing but wish me the best. All of them have given me their love and they have mine in return.

I N D E X

NOTE: AG refers to Alan C. Greenberg.

Abraham & Co., 16, 27
A.G. Becker, 57
airline stocks, 149–50
Allegheny Corporation, 17
Alletto, Lawrence, 152
Allied Stores, 109
Amazon.com, 68
American Express, 95–96
American International Group
  (AIG), 126, 189, 191
American Kennel Club, 65–66
American Museum of Natural
  History, 64–65, 121
American Red Cross, 54
American Viscose, 38
analysts, conference call with,
  154–55
Appleman, Nate, 13–14
archery: AG's interest in, 64
Asia, 111–13, 114, 134–35, 160. *See
  also specific nation*
Asset Management, Bear Stearns,
  129, 138–43
AT&T, 39–40
Aubry, Marcel, 24

Bache, 14, 78
Baker, Moe, 37, 38
Bank of America, 188, 190
Bank of New York Mellon, 190
Bankers Trust, 124

Banking Committee, U.S. Senate,
  193
bankruptcies. *See* Risk Arbitrage
  Department, Bear Stearns
bankruptcy; as option for Bear
  Stearns, 4, 6, 169, 178, 179, 180,
  182, 183
banks: and global financial
  crisis, 188–90; investment, 191,
  194–95. *See also specific bank*
Barclays, 188
Barnish, Keith, 152
Baruch, Bernard, 8
bathroom renovations: in Israel
  Museum, 118–19
Bear, Joseph, 18, 20, 34
Bear Stearns: bankruptcy as
  option for, 4, 6, 169, 178, 179,
  180, 182, 183; branch offices
  of, 48–49, 55, 69, 89, 111, 160;
  capitalization of, 46, 89; core
  principles of, 49, 69; culture at,
  45, 49, 70–78, 160, 192; debt of,
  3, 154–55, 160, 171, 180, 194;
  decentralized business model
  at, 157; decline of, 143, 144–48;
  demise of, 1–7, 168–85, 192;
  description of offices of, 16–17;
  expansion of, 1, 38, 48–49, 55,
  69, 76, 89, 108, 111–12, 115; as
  first casualty of global credit

201

Bear Stearns (*cont.*)
crisis, 191–92; founding of, 18; headquarters of, 55, 56, 76, 115–16; IPO of, 73–74, 77, 98–99, 103–4; job titles at, 104, 105–6; JPMorgan Chase buyout of, 5–7, 11, 148, 169, 177–85, 187, 191, 193, 194, 195; lenders of, 4, 173–74; liquidity of, 3, 4, 11, 61, 143, 150–51, 152, 154, 159, 160, 169, 172, 174, 175, 176, 177, 189; long-term/bank financing at, 173–74, 175, 176; management structure at, 103–4; milestone in rise of, 38; options on, 174; organization and hierarchy at, 49, 103–4; primary sources of income for, 33–34, 55, 89–90, 129, 149; profits and losses at, 4, 55–56, 99–100, 113, 114, 128–29, 142–43, 145, 157, 166, 170, 175–76; purpose/goal of, 2–3; ratings on, 3, 154–55, 171, 180, 194; repo financing at, 175, 176, 180; reputation of, 4, 19, 74, 81, 132, 136, 142; rumors about need of outside capital for, 159–60; stock buyback by, 150–51, 154, 164; stock price of, 3, 4, 128–29, 137, 145, 154, 155, 163, 164–65, 169, 170, 171, 174, 180, 184; stock splits and dividends of, 99. *See also specific person, department, or topic*
Begleiter, Steven, 152
Berkshire Hathaway, 126
Bernanke, Ben, 177, 178, 179, 182, 192–93
Black Monday (October 16, 1987), 75–78
Blackstone, Harry Sr., 62, 63
Blackstone Group, 151–52, 153
block trading, 33–34, 55–56, 151

board of directors, Bear Stearns, 1, 5–7, 100, 110, 165–66, 167, 178–85
Boesky, Ivan, 30
bonds: of airline companies, 150; Bear Stearns general corporate strategy for, 81–82; corporate, 114, 129; distressed, 109; long-term, 151; municipal, 81–84, 85–86, 129; in 1960s and 1970s, 81; ratings on, 138. *See also* mortgage-backed assets
booms-and-busts, 133–38
Boy Scouts of America, 63
Boys Club, 63
Breedon, Simon, 152
Brennan, Terry, 31
bridge financing, 108–9
bridge playing. *See* Cayne, James E. "Jimmy": as bridge player; Spector, Warren J.: as bridge player
Brooke, Edward, 26
Budge, Homer, 48
Buffett, Warren, 10, 126, 189
Bush, George W., 147, 163, 189
buyback, Bear Stearns. *See* stock buyback, Bear Stearns

Campeau, Robert, 109
Carey, Hugh, 82, 83, 84
Carl M. Loeb, 14, 16
Cayne, James E. "Jimmy": achievements of, 115–16; and AG on *The Apprentice*, 116; AG's morning ride arrangements with, 87; and AG's philanthropy, 117–18; AG's relationship with, 85, 88, 89, 103–4, 105, 110–11, 112, 113, 114, 116–18, 129, 146, 158, 165, 167; and AG's retirement, 127; and AG's role at Bear Stearns, 128; and airline holdings, 150; and analysts

conference call, 154–55; and
Asian/China business, 111,
112–13, 157–58, 159, 160–62;
and Blackstone-Hilton deal,
152, 153; as bridge player, 6, 80,
87–89, 113, 145, 147, 153–54,
158, 162, 163, 164, 172, 179;
and co-presidency, 104, 105–7;
commission on stock sales for,
185; company stock owned
by, 6, 145, 148, 149, 185; and
compensation committee,
110, 111; compensation for,
84–85, 111, 114, 130, 148, 149;
and demise of Bear Stearns,
6–7, 169, 172, 178–79, 183, 185;
disengagement of, 150; and El
Salvador bank deal, 145–46;
as executive board chairman,
6, 172; Gasparino comments
about, 86–87; Geithner
comments of, 118; as golfer,
153–54, 162; and hedge fund
portfolios, 141, 142, 153–54,
162–63; helicopter rides of,
152–53, 154–55, 163; hiring of,
80–81, 84–85; home of, 152–53;
image of, 163; and IPO, 103–4;
job titles for, 112, 160; ladder
ranking of, 102; and leveraged-
buyout financing, 149; and
LTCM, 124, 125–27; and
Madison Avenue headquarters
of Bear Stearns, 115–16; and
management structure, 103–4;
marijuana smoking by, 163,
164; Molinaro appointment by,
164, 165; named CEO, 112, 160;
named chairman of board of
directors, 167; named president,
105, 106–7; named president
and CEO, 122; nickname for,
129; and 1999 meltdown,
122; and NYC bonds, 85,
86; partnership for, 85; and
Perella deal, 114; personal and
professional background of, 80–
81; personality and character
of, 80, 81, 85, 86, 87, 88, 89, 102,
103, 104, 110–11, 144–46, 148,
153–54, 160, 163; philanthrophy
of, 145; political interests of,
147; power and control of, 162;
and private client services, 89,
102–3, 110; and profit-sharing
plan, 101–2; reputation of,
163–64; resignation of, 158, 164,
165–67, 169; resignation threats
of, 106; in retail department,
84–85; as scapegoat for failure
of Bear Stearns, 192; Schwartz's
relationship with, 132; and
Spector as bridge player,
131; Spector's relationship
with, 132, 144, 146–47; and
Spector's resignation, 154, 155;
and Spector's successor, 164;
and stock buyback, 150, 151;
successors to, 127, 147, 165–66;
Tang hiring by, 160; *Wall Street
Journal* story about, 162–64; and
Watkins, 129–30
Celanese Corporation, 40–41
Chase Manhattan Bank, 84,
124
cheating: AG's views about, 88
Chicago, Illinois: Bear Stearns
branch in, 48–49
children's holiday party, Bear
Stearns, 63
China, 111–12, 113, 134, 157–58,
159, 160–62
China CITIC Group, 157, 159,
160–62
Chrysler Corporation, 190
Cioffi, Ralph, 139, 150
Citibank/Citigroup, 84, 126,
145–46, 190

Classen High School (Oklahoma City), 12
clearing transactions, 56–57, 76, 89, 123
CNBC, 4, 172, 173, 174, 175, 176, 179
co-presidency: at Bear Stearns, 104, 105–7
Cogan, Berlind, Weill & Levitt, 50–52
Cohan, William D., 103
Cohen, H. Rodgin, 181, 183
collateralized debt obligations, 142
commissions, 54–55, 185
compensation committee. *See* management and compensation committee
compensation issues, 98, 100–102, 110, 113, 148–49, 165, 166. *See also* management and compensation committee; *specific person*
competition: Lewis' views about, 27
compliance officers, Bear Stearns, 73
Conopask, James, 152
corporate finance department, 57–58, 111
credit default swaps (CDSs), 174
credit-rating agencies, 135. *See also specific agency*
Credit Suisse, 78
Credit Suisse First Boston, 109
Crystal, Graef, 100–101

Daily Oklahoman: AG interception letter to, 96–97
Dallas Aces, 88
damage-control initiative, 154–55
Danzig, J. J., 18, 19

Davidson, Marvin, 41
Davis, Al, 22
deferred compensation, 148–49, 165
Delta Airlines, 150
derivatives, 129, 170, 188
Dickson, Leonard, 15, 17, 18, 21, 22
Diller, Barry, 115
Dimon, Jamie, 177–78, 182, 183
dogs: AG's love of, 65–66
dollar-averaging strategy, 35
dot.coms, 133–35, 136
Dow Jones Industrial Average, 15, 55, 75, 155
Drexel Burnham, 78
DuPont, 56
Dutch-auction tenders, 90–93
dwarfism, 121–22

E.F. Hutton, 78
Einbender, Alvin, 103
El Salvador bank deal, 145–46
elections, presidential, 147, 190–91
elevator, for Cayne, 146
Emergency Economic Stabilization Act, 189
Employee Stock Option Plan, Bear Stearns (ESOP), 99
employees, Bear Stearns: AG concerns about, 195; AG financial support for some, 195; AG meetings with new, 79–80; and Asian expansion, 113; Cayne fears about, 150; commission on stock trades for, 185; compensation for, 98, 100–102, 110, 113, 148–49, 165, 166; and demise of Bear Stearns, 6, 192, 195; and hedge funds, 139; and hiring/employment policies, 43–44, 49, 69–70; and JPMorgan buyout

of Bear Stearns, 184, 192, 195; layoffs of, 166; profit-sharing plan for, 99–100, 101–2; and size of workforce, 1, 89; stock ownership by, 6, 99, 184. *See also specific person*

Enron, 129

Equity Funding Corporation of America, 52–53

Esther Greenberg Junior High School (Har Gilo, Israel), 120

executive committee, Bear Stearns: AG as chairman of, 1, 127; and AG decision to name Cayne as president, 106–7; and AG responsibilities, 107–8; AG role in, 128; and Blackstone-Hilton deal, 151–52; and Cayne-AG relationship, 110–11, 116, 165; and Cayne resignation, 164, 165–66; and compensation issues, 100–101, 110, 166; and ESOP, 99; and hedge fund portfolios, 141–42, 150; and ladder rankings, 102; and LTCM, 124, 125; and management structure, 103–4; and partnership withdrawals, 46; power of, 110; and stock buyback, 150–51. *See also specific member*

Farland, Leo, 23–24

favors: AG views about, 53

Federal Deposit Insurance Corporation (FDIC), 189, 193, 194

Federal Home Loan Mortgage Corporation "Freddie Mac," 188, 190, 191

Federal National Mortgage Association "Fannie Mae," 187–88, 190, 191

Federal Reserve Bank, 5, 49, 126, 179–85, 189, 191, 192, 193, 194

Federal Reserve Bank, New York, 118, 124, 125, 177

Federated Department Stores, 109

Federation of Jewish Philanthropies, 54, 117

Finkle, David, 22–23, 31, 34

Finney, Howard, 82

First Boston, 78, 132

fishing: AG interest in, 63–64

Fisk, Jim, 8

fixed-income division, Bear Stearns, 129, 136, 137, 152, 155–57, 162, 164, 169

flash reports, 70–71

Flom, Joe, 92

football, 12, 13, 19, 25, 96

footpath loans, 109

Ford, Gerald, 82

Foreign Bondholders Protective Council, 24, 25

foreign department, Bear Stearns: Slade starts, 29

Fortune magazine: ratings of admired firms by, 136

Four Seasons Nursing Centers of America, 50, 115

4 percent rule, 53–54, 117

Fox, Freddy, 14

Frey, Melissa, 177

Fuld, Richard S. Jr., 193

Gasparino, Charles, 86–87

Geithner, Timothy, 118, 177, 178, 179, 180–81, 182

General Electric, 78

General Motors Corporation, 56, 190

Geoghan, Joseph, 152

Gilbride, John, 93

Glaser, David, 152

global financial crisis (2008), 187–88, 191–92
gold mining stock, 32
Goldman Sachs, 16, 27, 33, 55, 126, 132, 181, 188–89, 190, 194
Goldstein, Jerry, 47
Golsen, Jack, 50–51
Gould, Jay, 8
greed: AG views about, 133
Greenberg, Alan C. "Ace":
  ambitions of, 8, 22, 25, 46;
  broker's license for, 23; cancer of, 61–62, 144;as CEO, 104, 127; as chairman, 107–8, 112; childhood and youth of, 10–13, 21, 62, 63–64; clients of, 25–26, 174–75; company stock held by, 148–49; compensation for, 15, 31, 45–46, 114, 148–49; early career of, 9, 13–27; education of, 8, 9, 13, 14; family background of, 9–10, 42–43; leadership/management style of, 46, 48–49, 66–67, 70–78; milestone in career of, 38; nickname for, 13, 117; NYC housing arrangements of, 21–22, 30–31, 47, 108; partnership in Bear Stearns for, 33; personal/family life of, 62, 72, 87; personal interests of, 12–13, 62–63, 64–65; personal philosophy of, 111; personality and character of, 24, 35, 107; philanthropy of, 54, 63, 68–69, 117–22, 195; press descriptions of, 11; priorities of, 103; reputation of, 13, 74, 157; "resignation" of, 36–37; responsibilities at Bear Stearns of, 1, 107–8; retirements of, 127, 148–49; role at Bear Stearns of, 103, 106, 127, 128, 156, 158, 162; role models for, 8–9, 42–43, 127; seat-of-the-pants methodology of, 30; social life of, 14, 21–22, 23–24; strategic thinking about Bear Stears of, 45–46, 70; suspension for technical violation of, 32–33; thoughts of leaving Bear Stearns of, 158; titles at Bear Stearns for, 1, 104, 107–8, 112, 127; trading strategy of, 35–41, 46; typical workday of, 1–2; as vice chairman emeritus, 185; work ethic of, 30–31, 62
Greenberg, DiAnne (sister), 9, 43, 118, 119, 195
Greenberg, Esther Zeligson (mother), 9–10, 11, 12, 21, 22, 32, 62, 120
Greenberg, Kathryn Olson "Kathy" (wife), 72, 121, 122, 129, 134, 177, 196
Greenberg, Lynne (daughter), 196
Greenberg, Maynard (brother), 9, 11, 118–19, 195
Greenberg, Ted (father): advice from, 30, 35, 196–97; and AG cancer, 62; and AG childhood and youth, 12, 63–64; and AG move to NYC, 14; as AG role model, 42–43; employee relationships with, 45–46; family background of, 9–10; and gold mining stock, 32; Israeli sports center named for, 120; loan to AG from, 23; NYC visit of, 22; philanthropy of, 11, 53–54; professional career of, 10
Greenberg, Teddy (son), 144, 196
Greenberg Academy for Successful Aging, 121
Greenberg Center for Skeletal Dysplasias, 121, 122
Greenberg Grab, 64
Greenberg Honor System, 53
The Greenbrier (West Virginia), 20

Gruss, Joe, 38
Gulf+Western, 81
Gutfreund, John, 47, 87

H. Hentz, 14
"Haimchinkel" (Haimchinkel
  Malintz Anaynika), 66–67, 68,
  69, 75, 76, 97–98, 110–11, 139,
  170, 181
Har Gilo (Israel), 120
Harmonie Club, 59–60, 63
Hart, Kitty Carlisle, 8
Hayden, Stone & Company, 50–52
hedge funds: at Bear Stearns,
  4, 129, 138–43, 152, 153–54,
  156–57, 159, 162–63, 174, 176
Henry, Lonny, 152
High-Grade Structured Credit
  Strategies Enhanced Leverage
  Fund, 139–43
High-Grade Structured Credit
  Strategies Master Fund, 139–43
Hilton Hotels Corporation,
  151–52, 153
Hirsch, Eddie, 43
Hollywood Golf Club, 153
Horace Mann School (Oklahoma
  City), 11–12
Hospital for Special Surgery
  (HSS), 117, 120–21, 122
House of Cards (Cohan), 103, 105,
  106, 107, 112, 118, 158
housing bubble, 135–38
hunting: AG interest in, 64–65

IBM, 55
India, 134
insider trading, 53
institutional investors: Bear
  Stearns' block trading with,
  33–34; and commissions, 55;
  debt securities offered to,
  24–25; and dot.coms, 135; and
  JPMorgan buyout of Bear

Stearns, 184; and mortgage-
  backed securities, 139; and
  primary sources of income
  for Bear Stearns, 33–34; and
  "special offerings," 55–56
interception-statistic inspiration,
  96–97
International Monetary Fund
  (IMF), 122
Investment Banking Department,
  Bear Stearns, 72, 89, 149
investment banks, 191, 194–95
Investor Diversified Services,
  17–18, 20, 48
Israel: Maccabiah Games in, 88;
  philanthropy in, 118–19, 120
Israel Museum (Jerusalem),
  118–19

Japan: war debts of, 24–25
Jardine Matheson Group, 77–78
J.C. Flowers & Company, 181
Jewish Home and Hospital, 63
Johns Hopkins Hospital, 121–22
Josephthal & Co., 16, 27
J.P. Morgan, 124
JPMorgan Chase: AG takes
  position at, 185; buyout of
  Bear Stearns by, 5–7, 11, 148,
  169, 177–85, 187, 191, 193, 194,
  195; hiring of Bear Stearns
  employees by, 192, 195; and
  TARP, 190

Kaminsky, Peter, 64
Kedumim, Neot, 119
Kelly, Kate, 162–63
Kennedy, John F., 36
Kerry, John, 147
Keswick family, 77–78
Kidder Peabody, 78
Kinney National Services, Inc.,
  94–95
Klein, Gene, 86

Kohlberg, Jerome "Jerry," 57–59, 61, 132
Kohlberg, Kravis & Roberts, 59
Kollek, Teddy, 118–19, 120
Komansky, David, 125, 126
Kraft, Robert, 116
Kravis, Henry, 58–59
Kudlow, Lawrence, 132

ladder rankings, 102
Lasker, Bernard J. "Bunny," 33, 35, 51–52
Latin America: Bear Stearns business in, 111
Lay, Kenneth, 129
Lazard, 132, 181
leadership: AG views about, 42–43
Lebenthal & Company, 80
Lehman Brothers, 16, 124, 188, 191, 192–93, 194
Leval & Co., 24
leverage: AG views about, 108, 137; at Bear Stearns, 157, 162; and global credit crisis, 188; and hedge funds, 139–43; and JPMorgan buyout of Bear Stearns, 184; at Lehman, 193; and LTCM, 123
leveraged buyouts, 58, 149, 151–52
Levy, Dave, 30
Levy, Gus, 27, 33, 55
Lewis, Joe, 170, 184
Lewis, Salim L. "Cy": AG as assistant to, 34–41; and AG as head of risk arbitrage, 29; AG deal with, 36–41, 47; and AG desire for job in risk arbitrage, 18, 20–21; AG morning rides with, 47, 87; AG relationship with, 34, 36–41, 45; as AG role model, 42; and AG style and temperament, 107; and AG trading strategies, 35–41, 46, 72; and AT&T trade, 39–40; and block trading, 33–34; and Celanese bonds, 40–41; and commissions, 55; competitors comment of, 27; death of, 26, 47–48, 59–60, 66; estate of, 61; and Finkle, 22, 23; as head of risk arbitrage department, 18; impact on Bear Stearns of, 19, 60; initiation of risk arbitrage department by, 19–20, 22; and Investor Diversified Services trade, 17; Kohlberg relationship with, 57–58; Levy comment of, 27; and nepotism policy, 44–45; and NYC bond business, 85, 86; personality and character of, 19, 20, 33, 35, 47–48, 57–58; philanthropy and volunteerism of, 54; professional background of, 18; reputation of, 20; research views of, 30; retirement of, 59–60; as risk committee member, 39; role in Bear Stearns of, 45, 59; and Shin-Etsu deal, 25; talents of, 23, 33; trading strategy of, 23, 33, 35–41
Lewis, Sandy, 44–45
L.F. Rothschild, 78
Liman, Arthur, 77
Ling-Temco Vought, 81
Little People of America, 121
Loeb Rhoades, 55, 57
Loews, 81
Long-Term Capital Management (LTCM), 123–27, 192
losing positions: AG views about, 30, 71–72; burying of, 73; and compliance officers, 73; and LCTM, 123–27; Lewis views about, 33; Meriwether views about, 123; and trading strategies, 33, 34–36
Louis Dreyfus & Co., 24

Low, Ted, 18, 19, 20, 21, 26, 28, 44, 47, 56, 61, 66, 87
Lowenstein, Roger, 123
LSB Industries, Inc., 50

M.A. Shapiro & Company, 48
Maccabiah Games (Israel), 88
magic: AG interest in, 62–63
Malone, John, 115
management and compensation committee, Bear Stearns, 46, 100, 131, 141, 165
Marano, Tom, 162
Marshall, Everett, 11–12
martial arts, 63
Marx, Gene, 82
Mayer, Harold C. "Bill," 18, 19, 20, 37–38, 54, 80
Mayer, Jeffrey, 152, 162
Mayo Clinic, 62
MBA degrees, 69
McCain, John, 191
McKusick, Victor, 121
media: role in demise of Bear Stearns of, 4, 173
media conference, Bear Stearns, 172–73
Memos from the Chairman (Greenberg), 68, 78
mergers and acquisitions, 132
Meriwether, John, 123, 124–25, 126
Merrill Lynch, 48, 49, 124–25, 188, 194
Missouri Pacific Railroad, 26–27
mistakes: AG's views about, 24, 42
Mitsubishi, 189
Molinaro, Samuel L. Jr., 142, 150–52, 154, 155, 164–65, 166, 172, 174, 177–79
Moody's, 3, 171, 180
moral hazard, 191
Morgan Guaranty, 84
Morgan, J. P., 8, 9

Morgan Stanley, 92, 93, 114, 124, 188–89, 190, 194
mortgage-backed assets, 4, 5, 89, 135–43, 154, 156–57, 164, 166, 170, 171, 182
Mortgage-Backed Bond Trading Department, Bear Stearns, 114
motivational messages, AG's, 66–68
Municipal Assistance Corporation (MAC), 84, 85
municipal bonds, 81–84, 85–86, 129
mutual funds, 114

Nabors Industries, 147–48
National Amusements, 114
nepotism, 43–45
New York City: AG early days in, 13–15, 21–22; AG housing arrangements in, 21–22, 30–31, 47, 108; municipal bonds of, 81–84, 85–86
New York State: and UDC bonds, 82–84
New York Stock Exchange: clearing transactions for, 57; commissions for trades on, 54–55; and Equity Funding deal, 52–53; and Hayden, Stone deal, 50–52; Lasker chairmanship of, 33, 51–52; Lewis seat on, 19; special trust fund of, 49–52; trading volume on, 15
New York Times, 2, 64, 76, 93, 96, 112, 117
New York University: AG gifts to, 68–69, 121
1998 panic, 124
1999 meltdown, 122
Nixon, Richard, 51
"Nookie" (Itzhak Nanook Pumpernickanaylian), 67, 68, 69
Northwest Airlines, 150

Obama, Barack, 190, 191
Ohio Mattress Company, 109
Oil and Gas Department, Bear
Stearns, 14–15, 16–21
Oklahoma City, Oklahoma: AG
vacation in, 32; Greenberg
family home in, 8–13, 14
Olson, Kathryn. *See* Greenberg,
Kathryn Olson
online discount brokers, 31–32, 55
outside consultants: AG views
about, 108
Overlander, Craig, 152
overnight borrowing, 4, 176
Owens, Jimmy, 12

Paget, Stephen, 121
Paine Webber, 109
paper-clip-envelope-rubber-band
schemes, 74
Paramount Pictures, 114
Parr, Gary, 181, 183
partnerships, Bear Stearns:
compensation for, 110; and
effects of partners' deaths on
corporation, 61; and ESOP
contributions, 99; and IPO, 98–
99; limited, 26, 68; and partners
keeping in touch, 67–68, 153;
and partnership investments in
corporation, 46–47; retirement
of, 98. *See also* senior managing
directors; *specific person*
Paulson, Henry, 177, 178, 179,
180–81, 182, 183, 190
Pepsi-Cola North America, 116
Perella, Joseph, 113–14
Petito, Frank, 92
P.F. Fox, 9, 14
Pfizer, 117
philanthropy, 53–54, 68–69, 73,
105, 117–22, 145, 195. *See also*
specific person
power: AG views about, 103

private client services, 89, 102–3,
110
profit-sharing plan, employee,
99–100, 101–2
Prudential, 78
PSDs, 69–70, 75, 80, 102
Public Library, New York, 14, 121

Rabobank Group, 173
railroad industry: Lewis interest
in, 22
ratings: on Bear Stearns corporate
debt, 3, 154–55, 171, 180, 194
ratings agencies, 138. *See also*
specific agency
real estate boom-and-bust, 4,
135–38, 188, 190, 193
Redstone, Sumner, 114–15
Regan, Don, 48
Reiff, Randy, 152
Reisinger Trophy, 88
repurchase-agreement financing
(repos), 175, 176, 180
Research Department, Bear
Stearns, 30, 55, 131, 132
Retail Operations, Bear Stearns,
48–49, 71, 79, 84–85, 89, 111
Reuben's Restaurant (New York
City), 63
Rhoades & Co., 14, 16
Ribicoff, Abraham, 127
Ring, Gus, 25–26, 32, 68
risk: AG views about, 2
risk arbitrage: AG mentors
concerning, 33; definition of,
26–27; in 1950s, 29
Risk Arbitrage Department,
Bear Stearns: AG approach
to trading in, 30; AG as head
of, 29–34; AG builds client
base in, 25–26; AG early days
with, 22–27; AG transfer to, 18,
20–21; and Investors Diversified
Services trade, 17–18, 20; and

Lewis-AG deal, 36–41; Lewis as head of, 18; Lewis starts, 19–20, 22; Lewis strategy for, 23, 33; as major source of income for Bear Stearns, 33, 39, 55; opportunities for young people in, 19–20

risk committee, Bear Stearns, 39, 71, 108, 128, 137, 140, 156, 157

Roberts, George, 58–59

Robinson, James, 95–96

Rosenwald, John "Johnny": AG as housemate of, 31; AG morning rides with, 47, 87; and AT&T trade, 39–40; Cayne phone call to, 106–7; and Cayne story of dissolving of co-presidency, 107; as co-president, 104, 105–7; and commissions, 57; and corporate finance, 57; and Dutch-auction idea, 92; at JPMorgan Chase, 185; and Kinney IPO, 94; and Kohlberg activities, 59; and Lewis personality, 48; and management structure, 103; martial arts lessons of, 63; named vice chairman, 105; and naming Cayne as president, 106; and nepotism policy, 44; and partnership investments in Bear Stearns, 46; personality and character of, 57; philanthrophic interests of, 105; and retail expansion, 48; and salaries and bonuses at Bear Stearns, 45; as vice chairman emeritus, 185

Ross, Steve, 39, 94–95

Rothschild, L. F., 27

Royal Dutch Company, 29

Rudd-Melikian, 37

Russia, 109–10, 122

Salomon Brothers, 18, 47, 123

Salomon Smith Barney, 124, 126

Sarno, Herman, 21

Sarno, Jay, 13, 21

Sartorius, 14

Savio, Kenny, 145, 148, 172, 177

scapegoats: for Bear Stearns demise, 192

Schiff, Jacob, 8–9

Schlesinger, Hans. *See* Slade, John

scholarship funds, 68–69

Schwartz, Alan D.: and AG intention to retire, 158; AG views about, 129, 130, 168–69, 173; and Blackstone-Hilton deal, 152; Cayne relationship with, 132; and Cayne resignation, 165–66; as Cayne successor, 127, 147, 165–66; CNBC interview of, 175, 176; as co-president and co-COO, 127, 132; and demise of Bear Stearns, 5–6, 168–70, 175, 176, 177, 178, 179, 180, 181, 185; on executive committee, 132; as head of investment banking department, 72; and hedge fund portfolios, 142; hiring of, 131; and JPMorgan buyout of Bear Stearns, 5–6, 177, 178, 179, 180, 181, 185; at media conference, 172–73; and mortgage-backed assets, 170; personality and character of, 132; professional career of, 131–32; Spector relationship with, 132; and Spector resignation, 155; and stock buyback, 151; and trading limits, 72–73

seat-of-the-pants methodology, AG's, 30

Securities and Exchange Commission (SEC), 49, 92

securities violations, 32–33
self-policing initiatives, 70–71
senior managing directors:
    and Cayne resignation, 165;
    company stock held by, 148–49,
    157; compensation for, 98,
    100–101, 148; and IPO, 98;
    keeping in touch with, 153;
    philanthropy of, 117. *See also
    specific person*
Shapiro, Morris, 48
shareholders: and JPMorgan
    buyout of Bear Stearns, 5, 184,
    185, 187
Shin-Etsu Chemical Company,
    24–25, 26
Sills, Beverly, 127
Singleton, Henry, 92
60 Minutes (CBS-TV), 192–93
Skadden, Arps, 92
Slade, John, 18, 21, 25, 28–29,
    34–35
Slydini, 63, 87–88
Smith Barney, 49
Smith, Kay, 121–22
smoking, 146
"special offerings," 55–56
Spector, Warren J.: AG
    relationship with, 155–56; AG
    views about, 129, 130, 138;
    and Blackstone-Hilton deal,
    152; as bridge player, 130–31,
    147, 153–54; and Cayne-AG
    relationship, 116; Cayne
    relationship with, 132, 144,
    146–47; as Cayne successor, 127,
    147; Cayne views about, 147; as
    co-president and co-COO, 127,
    132; compensation for, 130; and
    El Salvador bank deal, 145–46;
    on executive committee, 116,
    131; fixed-income knowledge
    of, 155–57; and hedge fund
    portfolios, 141, 142, 153–54;

hiring of, 130; and LTCM, 125;
    on management committee,
    131; and mortgage-backed
    securities, 137, 139; and Nabors
    Industries deal, 147–48; named
    senior managing director, 131;
    nickname for, 130; personal and
    professional background of,
    130; personality and character
    of, 130, 132, 148; political
    interests of, 147; resignation of,
    154, 155, 162; responsibilities
    of, 129; and risk committee,
    128; as scapegoat for failure of
    Bear Stearns, 192; Schwartz
    relationship with, 132; and
    stock buyback, 151; strengths
    of, 130; successors to, 162,
    164
sports: AG interest in, 12–13
Standard & Poor's, 154, 180
State Street Bank, 190
Stearns, Robert B., 18–19, 34
Steel, Johannes, 32
steel industry, 36
Steinberg, Robert "Bobby," 72–73,
    152
Stewart, James, 193
Stewart, Mark Sr., 44–45
stock buyback, Bear Stearns,
    150–51, 154, 164
stock warrants, 93–96
Stoops, Bob, 97
Strauss, Bob, 109–10
Street's (clothing store), 10–11,
    45–46, 196
subprime loans, 137, 142, 188
Sullivan & Cromwell, 181
Supreme Court, U.S.: Missouri
    Pacific decision of, 27

Tang, Donald, 160
Tannin, Matthew, 139
Tarnopol, Mickey, 103

Ted Greenberg Sports Center (Har Gilo, Israel), 120
TED (Technology, Entertainment, Design) conference: AG at, 134
Teledyne, 92
ten-minute rule, 67
tender offers, 90–93
The Apprentice (TV show), 116
theGlobe.com, 133–34
Theory of Relativity, AG's, 8
Thomson MacKinnon, 78
Todd Shipyards, 92–93
"too big to fail," 191
trading limits, 72–73
trading rooms: clients in, 31–32
Treasury Department, U.S., 5, 49, 93, 188, 189, 192, 193, 194
Troubled Asset Relief Program (TARP), 189–90
Trump, Donald, 116
trust: AG belief in importance of, 3
20th Century-Fox, 95

Unilever, 116
United Jewish Appeal, 54
United Light and Railway, 23
University of Missouri, 8, 13, 121
University of Oklahoma, 8, 12, 13, 97, 121, 196
University of Wisconsin: AG at, 14
Upton, Robert, 177

Urban Coalition, 54
Urban Delevopment Corporation (UDC), 81–84

Vanity Fair: Bear Stearns story in, 11
venture capitalists, 134
Viacom, 114
Viagra, 117, 118, 121
Volga Auto Works, 109

Wahrsager, Sig, 57, 59
Wall Street Journal, 2, 93, 157, 162–64
Warner Bros.-Seven Arts, 94
Warner Communications, 39, 94–95
Wasserstein, Bruce, 113
Watkins, Sherron, 129–30
Weill, Sandy, 126
Wells Fargo, 190
Wertheim, 14
whistle-blowing, 73–74
Whittemore, Fred, 92
Williams, Ted, 31
Workman Publishing, 68
World Bank, 122

Young Men's Hebrew Association, 54
Young, Robert, 17–18, 20
Young Women's Hebrew Association, 54